Dairy Delicious

The Sour Cream/Yogurt/Buttermilk Cookbook

Dedication

This book is dedicated to families and friends and to the memory of Dash, who loved to drink buttermilk.

From Dot and Twinkle Toes

by Louise Bailey & Madeline Wright

Front Cover — Cold Buttermilk Soup, page 30

Dairy Delicious
by
Louise Bailey and Madeline Wright

First Printing — May, 1988
Second Printing — August, 1988

Dairy Delicious Publishing Limited
Box 293, Station "G"
Calgary, Alberta, Canada
T3A 2G2

Canadian Cataloguing in Publication Data
Bailey, Louise, 1948-
Dairy delicious

Includes index.
ISBN 0-919845-55-X

1. Cookery (Sour cream and milk). 2. Cookery (Yogurt).
I. Wright, Madeline, 1923- II. Title.
TX759.B34 1988 641.6'7 C88-098074-3

Photography by:
Ross C. (Hutch) Hutchinson
Hutchinson & Company Commercial Photography Ltd.
Calgary, Alberta

Madeline Wright's portrait by:
Russ Robinson Photographer
Southampton, Ontario

Dishes, Accessories and Services Compliments of:
Bowering, Market Mall, Calgary
Kensington Kitchen Co., Kensington Crescent, Calgary
Tina Komonko, Port Elgin, Ontario
John Kurta, Calgary
Woodward Stores Limited, Market Mall, Calgary

Designed, Printed and Produced in Canada by:
Centax
Publishing Consultant and Food Stylist — Margo Embury
Designer — Blair Fraser
1048 Fleury Street, Regina, Saskatchewan, Canada S4N 4W8
(306) 359-3737

Table of Contents

Emergency Substitutions

1 cup (250 mL) buttermilk	=	1 cup (250 mL) sour milk, OR 1 cup (250 mL) sweet milk plus 1 tbsp. (15 mL) vinegar or lemon juice
1 cup (250 mL) sour cream	=	1 cup (250 mL) yogurt
1 cup (250 mL) milk	=	1 cup (250 mL) yogurt plus 1/2 tsp. (2 mL) baking soda added to the flour in the recipe
1 cup (250 mL) buttermilk	=	⅞ cup skim milk plus 2 tbsp. commercial buttermilk (leave on counter overnight)

Foreword

This book has been a long time in the making. Many years ago a young bride asked her mother what to do with the leftover sour cream, after having baked potatoes. Since then, Mother and I have made, saved and adapted many recipes. Yogurt and buttermilk were added to our collection.

During the 1960's and 70's mother wrote a column entitled "Mainly for Women" for our hometown newspaper in which she shared many recipes and hints with her readers. Friends and relatives teased her about being an excellent cook, yet never having the time to write a cookbook. In the early 1980's, after a series of strokes, mother became a handi-capable person. A major portion of her rehabilitation was due to her strong desires to be back in her own kitchen and to be writing. This new phase of her life has allowed us to concentrate our efforts on producing this collection of recipes to share with you. Even though we are now hundreds of miles apart, Mother and I have taken great pleasure in working together on this project. It is our hope that some of our favorites will become some of yours.

It has long been our belief that dairy products are an important part of a healthy diet. Sour cream, yogurt and buttermilk offer a delicious addition to milk and cheese in fulfilling daily nutritional requirements.

Today, perhaps more than ever, people are conscious of the need for proper nutrition and the importance of dairy products, fruits, vegetables, meats and fiber in their diets, accompanied by regular excercise. At the same time, people want to be pampered with a special treat.

This book contains delicious and healthful yogurt-based appetizers, soups, main courses and desserts combined with luscious sour cream recipes and light, tangy buttermilk recipes. Dairy Delicious will appeal to the health conscious as well as those looking for downright decadent desserts. It is always nice to know that what you are eating is good for you too!

Best of all, when you want a Sour Cream, Yogurt or Buttermilk recipe you can conveniently look in this book and find it.

This book has been designed with both the family and entertaining in mind. Mealtimes are important times to communicate with family and friends. Make sure that you make time to eat together.

Bon Appetit!

Acknowledgement

We wish to extend special thanks to Margo Embury of Centax for her excellent guidance, to Linda Pap for proofreading and always being positive, and to Rick, Christine, Lea-Ann and Richard for their love and assistance, without which, this book would not have been possible.

The Cultured Club

Buttermilk, sour cream and yogurt are good sources of protein and calcium, which is so necessary in maintaining strong, healthy bones and teeth. Calcium also plays a vital role in helping to maintain normal muscle, nerve and circulatory functions.

Buttermilk

Buttermilk is *skim or 2% milk* treated with a bacterial culture. The result is a sour, creamy refreshing taste. Buttermilk contains more lactic acid than skim milk and is more easily digested. Buttermilk used to be made from the residue left after buttermaking — hence the name.

Sour Cream

Sour cream is *sweet cream* to which a culture has been added. It is then allowed to ripen to a tart, rich flavor. It is not cream that has soured! It adds a rich creaminess to dips and sauces. Foods baked with it are moist and light. A new light version is now on the market.

Yogurt

Yogurt is *milk (whole or skim)* cultured with live bacteria. It is more easily digested than milk. Yogurt helps to maintain beneficial bacteria in the body. Some research suggests that yogurt may be beneficial in lowering cholesterol levels. Yogurt can be substituted for sour cream in any of these recipes to provide a more calorie-reduced recipe.

Yogurt, sour cream and buttermilk have been used for centuries by various cultures. As a matter of fact, yogurt is consumed in almost all parts of the world. Many people claim that yogurt has beneficial and healthful properties — from aiding digestion to treating high cholesterol levels. Sour cream, although highest in fat content, is a source of Vitamin A, protein, and potassium as well as calcium. Sour cream and buttermilk have played an important roll in European cuisine. Many people attest to the healthful properties of buttermilk. These calcium rich products can play an important roll in satisfying daily calcium requirements, thereby helping to prevent osteoporosis.

Dips, Spreads, Sauces & Dressings

Crunchy Spinach Dip

This dip is always a hit. Recipes given to you by friends bring back special memories.

10 oz.	pkg. frozen spinach, thawed, squeezed and chopped	283 g
8 oz.	can water chestnuts, drained and finely chopped	227 mL
1½ cups	sour cream	375 mL
½ cup	mayonnaise	125 mL
1.5-1.9 oz.	pkg. dry Vegetable Soup Mix	40-54 g
1	round loaf of bread as container (optional)	1

Combine all ingredients, except bread, and mix well. Cover and refrigerate overnight. To serve, hollow out unsliced pumpernickel, sourdough, or health round loaf and fill with the dip. Serve with bread pieces, raw vegetables and/or crackers. This dip can also be used as a spread on crackers or bread rounds.

Variation: Add ¼ cup (50 mL) finely chopped red onion to the dip. Garnish the serving tray with sprigs of parsley to freshen the breath.

Yield: Approximately 4 cups (4 L).

Tangy Worcestershire Dip

Worcestershire sauce adds a nice zip to this dip.

1 cup	mayonnaise	250 mL
1 cup	sour cream OR yogurt	250 mL
2 tbsp.	Worcestershire sauce	30 mL
1	garlic clove, minced	1
½ tsp.	ground oregano	2 mL
½ tsp.	thyme	2 mL
½ tsp.	dill weed	2 mL
2 tbsp.	freshly chopped parsley (optional)	30 mL

Mix well and refrigerate overnight. Serve with a colorful variety of raw vegetables.

Yield: Approximately 2 cups (500 mL).

Cottage Cheese Yogurt Dip

Tasty as a low-cal dip or dressing.

½ cup	cottage cheese	125 mL
½ cup	plain yogurt	125 mL
3 tbsp.	chopped green onion	45 mL
2 tbsp.	finely chopped dill pickle	30 mL
dash	cayenne pepper	dash

Blend cottage cheese and yogurt in a blender or with an electric beater until smooth. Fold in the green onion, dill pickle and cayenne. Serve with your favorite raw vegetables.

Yield: Approximately 1 cup (250 mL).

Mixed Garden Vegetable Dip

A colorful dip with interesting texture combinations.

1 cup	sour cream	250 mL
1 cup	yogurt	250 mL
½ cup	mayonnaise	125 mL
2 cups	finely chopped cucumber	500 mL
⅓ cup	thinly sliced green onions	75 mL
⅓ cup	shredded carrots	75 mL
⅓ cup	finely chopped radishes	75 mL
⅓ cup	finely chopped green pepper	75 mL
	salt and pepper to taste	

In a large bowl, blend all ingredients; mix well. Cover; refrigerate for several hours to blend. Serve with vegetables, chips or crackers.

Yield: Approximately 4 cups (4 L).

Egg Salad

A creamy mixture for rolls or sandwiches. This can also be served as an appetizer, on thinly sliced rye bread, garnished with fresh dill.

3	hard-cooked eggs, mashed	3
3 tbsp.	sour cream	45 mL
1 tbsp.	finely chopped green pepper	15 mL
1 tsp.	finely chopped onion	5 mL
1 tsp.	prepared mustard	5 mL
	salt and pepper to taste	

Combine all ingredients and blend well. Spread on rolls or bread.

Yield: 1 cup (250 mL).

Sour Cream Herb Dip

So easy to make and so tasty!

1 cup	sour cream	250 mL
1 cup	mayonnaise	250 mL
1 tbsp.	chopped parsley	15 mL
½ tsp.	crushed dill weed	2 mL
1 tsp.	minced onion	5 mL
½ tsp.	garlic powder	2 mL
drop	Tabasco sauce	drop

In a small bowl, combine all ingredients. Mix well and chill for several hours. Serve with crisp fresh vegetables and/or chips.

Yield: 2 cups (500 mL).

Avocado Dip

2	avocados, peeled and mashed	2
1 tbsp.	lemon juice	15 mL
¼ cup	sour cream OR yogurt	50 mL
¼ cup	mayonnaise	50 mL
5	bacon slices, crisply cooked and crumbled	5
¼ cup	finely chopped green onion	50 mL
dash	Tabasco sauce	dash

Combine avocado, lemon juice, sour cream and mayonnaise. Add bacon, green onion and Tabasco. Mix well. Chill thoroughly. Serve as a dip with tortilla chips and/or vegetables. Serve as a sauce on tacos. Serve on buns with sliced tomatoes, alfalfa sprouts and cheese slices.

Yield: 1 cup (250 mL).

Jalapeño Cheese Dip

This tasty Mexican treat will disappear before your eyes!

¼ lb.	medium OR old Cheddar cheese, shredded, approximately 1 cup (250 mL) well-packed	115 g
¾ cup	sour cream	175 mL
¼ cup	mayonnaise	50 mL
¼ cup	finely chopped green onion	50 mL
1-2	garlic cloves, minced	1-2
2 OR more	jalapeño peppers (tops removed and seeded), finely chopped	2 OR more

Thoroughly mix all the ingredients in an ovenproof dish. Bake at 275°F (140°C) for 15-20 minutes, or until the dip is completely warmed. Do not boil. Stir before serving to blend the melted cheese. Serve warm with corn chips and crisp vegetables.

Yield: 2 cups (500 mL).

Use decorative and innovative containers such as hollowed out fruits, vegetables, breads, rolls and pastry shells when serving dips.

Blue Cheese Dip Or Spread

For blue cheese fans, this will hit the spot.

1 cup	sour cream	250 mL
1 cup	mayonnaise	250 mL
4 oz.	blue cheese, crumbled	115 g
1 tsp.	chopped red onion	5 mL
¼ tsp.	garlic powder	1 mL
1/8 tsp.	paprika	0.5 mL
dash	oregano	dash
dash	Tabasco sauce	dash

Combine all of the ingredients, mixing by hand. Chill for 2 hours to allow flavors to blend. Serve with raw vegetables and/or crackers.

Yield: Approximately 2½ cups (625 mL).

Curry Dip

1 cup	yogurt	250 mL
1 cup	mayonnaise	250 mL
1 tbsp.	ketchup	15 mL
2 tsp.	chopped green onions	10 mL
½-1 tsp.	curry powder	2-5 mL
1/8 tsp.	garlic powder	0.5 mL
¼ tsp.	Worcestershire sauce	1 mL
dash	ginger	dash

In a small bowl, combine all ingredients. Cover; refrigerate several hours or overnight to blend flavors. Serve with raw vegetables.

Yield: Approximately 2 cups (500 mL).

Hummus With Yogurt

A very popular Middle Eastern dip, with a subtle tangy flavor. Don't just read this recipe - try it! Chick peas are good for you!

19 oz.	can garbanzo beans (chick peas), rinsed and drained	540 mL
5-6 tbsp.	plain yogurt	75-90 mL
2 tbsp.	olive oil	30 mL
2	green onions, chopped	2
2	large garlic cloves, chopped	2
½	lemon, juice of	½
	salt	
	freshly ground pepper	
	pita bread	
	tomato, avocado, alfalfa sprouts, red onion, cheese, hard-boiled eggs and/or bacon bits for garnish (optional)	

Purée first 8 ingredients in a food processor or blender. Refrigerate for several hours. Spread on pita bread. Add any combination of the following: a few slices of tomato, avocado slices, alfalfa sprouts, chopped red onion, shredded cheese or sliced eggs and bacon bits. Or use pita pieces for dipping into a bowl of Hummus. Spread can be refrigerated for up to 1 week.

Yield: 1½ cups (375 mL).

Recent research indicates that beans, including garbanzo beans, contain substances that are important in our diets to help protect against cancer.

Layered Shrimp Dip

This is a colorful and delicious addition to any entertaining menu.

8 oz.	cream cheese, softened	250 g
¼ cup	sour cream	50 mL
½ cup	seafood sauce	125 mL
4½ oz.	can shrimp, slightly mashed	114 mL
1 tsp.	lemon juice	5 mL
3 tbsp.	chopped green onion	45 mL
3 tbsp.	each chopped green and red pepper (optional)	45 mL
4-6	olives, sliced (optional)	4-6

Beat cream cheese and sour cream until fluffy. Spread on a serving plate. Spread seafood sauce over cream cheese. Sprinkle shrimp over sauce. Sprinkle lemon juice over shrimp. Top with green onion and add peppers and olives if desired. Serve with crackers or vegetables.

Serves: 8-12.

Smoked Salmon Dip

½ cup	smoked salmon bits	125 mL
1 cup	sour cream OR yogurt	250 mL
½ cup	cream cheese	125 mL
¼ cup	chopped Spanish onion	50 mL
½ tsp.	dill weed	2 mL
	pepper to taste	

Combine all ingredients in a food processor or blender and process until smooth. Serve with crackers or thinly sliced rye bread.

Yield: 2 cups (500 mL).

Smoked Salmon Coeur à la Crème

A truly elegant appetizer!

8 oz.	cream cheese, softened	250 g
1 cup	sour cream	250 mL
4 oz.	smoked salmon	113 g
¼ cup	chopped green onion	50 mL
1	garlic clove, minced	1
1½ tsp.	dill weed	7 mL

Beat cream cheese until fluffy; beat in sour cream, then salmon, onion, garlic and dill weed with blender or food processor. Line a 7" (18 cm) wide heart-shaped coeur à la crème mold that holds about 3½ cups (875 mL) or similar-sized wicker basket with a double layer of moistened cheesecloth. Fill with cheese mixture; press down, and cover. Set mold in a shallow pan to drain (if using a wicker basket, set on a wire rack, then in a pan). Refrigerate at least overnight (twenty-four to thirty-six hours is fine). Unmold onto a serving plate, lined with thinly sliced cucumber in overlapping circles; remove cheesecloth. Garnish with dill sprigs and lemon twists. Serve with crackers, bread or cucumber slices.

Serves: 6-10.

Variation: Adding finely chopped red and/or green pepper adds additional interest to this lovely appetizer.

For those extra special appetizer trays, use cookie cutters to shape bread or cucumber canapés.

Chocolate Sour Cream Sauce, page 22
Peanut Butter and Honey Dip, page 21
Marshmallow Sour Cream Sauce, page 23
Crème Fraîche, page 21
Chocolate Coeur à la Crème, page 20

Salmon Yogurt Spread

7½ oz.	can salmon	225 g
2 tbsp.	plain yogurt	30 mL
1 tbsp.	finely chopped fresh dill	15 mL
¼ tsp.	tarragon	1 mL
pinch	each salt and pepper	pinch

Drain salmon and mash, including the bones. Stir in the remaining ingredients. Refrigerate until ready to spread on bread or crackers. Alternately, serve on a lettuce leaf for a luncheon treat.

Yield: 1 cup (250 mL).

Seafood Canapés

4 oz.	can crab meat OR canned shrimp, drained and rinsed	115 g
2 tbsp.	lemon juice	30 mL
dash	pepper	dash
dash	cayenne pepper	dash
2 tbsp.	yogurt OR sour cream	30 mL
1 tbsp.	mayonnaise	15 mL
3	long English cucumbers	3
	parsley, paprika and black caviar	

Flake the crab meat or shrimp and toss with lemon juice, pepper, cayenne, yogurt and mayonnaise. Refrigerate. In the meantime, peel the cucumbers and cut into 1" (2.5 cm) rounds. Scoop out a small well in the center of each cucumber slice and place some of the seafood mixture in the well. Garnish with a variety of small fresh parsley sprigs, a dash of paprika or black caviar. Serve cold.

Yield: 24-36 canapés.

Crab Dip

Delicious as a dip or hot appetizer.

4 oz.	can crab meat	113 g
1 cup	mayonnaise	250 mL
½ cup	yogurt	125 mL
1 tbsp.	lemon juice	15 mL
	pepper to taste	
2 tbsp.	finely chopped green onions OR parsley (optional)	30 mL

Thoroughly combine all ingredients. Chill at least 2 hours before serving with assorted crackers.

Yield: 2 cups (500 mL).

Variation: Grilled Crab Rolls - spread the Crab Dip on Parkerhouse rolls (or your favorite roll). Broil until bubbly and warmed through. Watch carefully. Serve these appetizers warm.

Hot Crab Meat Dip

8 oz.	cream cheese	250 g
½ cup	sour cream	125 mL
½ tsp.	flour (optional)	2 mL
2 tbsp.	mayonnaise	30 mL
½	lemon, juice of	½
	pepper to taste	
7 oz.	can crab meat	200 g
dash	cayenne pepper	dash

Hot Crab Meat Dip (Cont'd.)

Soften and cream cheese well. Add remaining ingredients, except the crab meat and cayenne. Cut crab into small pieces and stir into cream cheese mixture. Bake at 400°F (200°C) for 15-20 minutes. Sprinkle with dash of cayenne pepper. Serve hot with assorted crackers.

Yield: Approximately 2 cups (500 mL).

Creamy Cheese Balls

These cheese balls freeze well and are wonderful on a cheese tray.

8 oz.	cream cheese, softened	250 g
3 cups	grated medium OR old Cheddar cheese	750 mL
¼ cup	sour cream	50 mL
⅓ cup	chopped green onions	75 mL
dash	Worcestershire sauce	dash
dash	cayenne pepper	dash
2 tsp.	chopped parsley (optional)	10 mL
½ cup	finely chopped pecans, walnuts OR almonds	125 mL

Thoroughly blend all ingredients, except the nuts. Divide into 2 balls. Roll in the chopped nuts. Wrap loosely in wax paper and chill for 2-3 hours before serving with assorted crackers.

Serves: 8-10.

Variation: Grilled Cheddar Buns - spread cheese mixture (with or without nuts) on roll or bagel halves. Broil until bubbly and hot. Watch closely. May be cut in half for appetizers.

Yield: 16 or more depending on size of bun.

Chocolate Coeur à la Crème

4 oz.	cream cheese	125 g
½ cup	plain yogurt	125 mL
1 tsp.	vanilla	5 mL
⅓ cup	semisweet chocolate chips, melted	75 mL

Beat cream cheese until fluffy. Add yogurt, vanilla and melted chocolate chips. Beat until smooth, creamy and well blended. Place moist cheesecloth, 2 layers thick, in each of 2 small coeur à la crème molds. Pour cheese sauce into mold. Cover with cheesecloth. Press sauce firmly into mold. Place on a plate on the counter for approximately 24 hours. Mixture will drain slightly. Refrigerate until serving time. Unmold onto a serving plate or cheese tray. Garnish with a piece of fruit such as an orange segment or strawberry fan and mint leaves. Serve with a variety of fruits and crackers.

Yield: Approximately 1½ cups (375 mL).

See photograph on page 16A.

Fruit'n'Dips

	select a variety of seasonal fresh fruits	
	lemon juice	
1 cup	yogurt OR sour cream	250 mL
1 cup	brown sugar	250 mL

Sprinkle fruits as necessary, with lemon juice to prevent browning. Arrange the fruit attractively on a serving tray. Place the yogurt and brown sugar in separate dishes, with serving spoons. Dip the fruit pieces in yogurt and sprinkle with sugar or provide a variety of the following dips.

Crème Fraîche

1 cup	whipping cream	250 mL
¼ cup	yogurt, sour cream OR buttermilk	50 mL

Gently combine the whipping cream and yogurt in a clean dish or jar. Cover and leave on the counter approximately 24 hours. Refrigerate for at least 12 hours, then, when sufficiently thickened, serve with a variety of dipping fruits. (Buttermilk may not thicken as much or as quickly as the yogurt or sour cream.)

Yield: Approximately 1¼ cups (300 mL).

See photograph on page 16A.

Peanut Butter and Honey Dip

¼ cup	peanut butter	50 mL
4 tbsp.	liquid honey	60 mL
2 tbsp.	orange juice	30 mL
½ cup	plain yogurt	125 mL

Combine the peanut butter and honey. Thoroughly mix in the orange juice and yogurt with electric blender until well blended. Refrigerate. Serve cold with fresh fruit and crackers.

Yield: Approximately 1 cup (250 mL).

See photograph on page 16A.

Fruit with Chocolate Sour Cream Sauce

The sour cream and chocolate combination adds a tart, yet refreshing taste.

1 cup	semisweet chocolate chips	250 mL
1½ cups	sour cream	375 mL
½ tsp.	cinnamon	2 mL
½ tsp.	vanilla	2 mL
4	bananas	4
2 cups	strawberries	500 mL
	chocolate curls for garnish	

Melt the chocolate chips then cool slightly. Gradually stir in the sour cream, cinnamon and vanilla. Refrigerate. Slice the bananas and toss with the strawberries. Place the fruit into 6 fruit dishes; top with chocolate sauce and garnish with a chocolate curl.

Yield: 2½ cups sauce.

Variation: Use sauce as an icing on tortes or cakes, or layer, in stacks 4 high, with graham wafer squares. Refrigerate overnight for a tart cheesecake-like treat. Make sure you ice the top and sides. This sauce is also delicious as a dip for fresh fruit.

See photograph on page 16A.

Marshmallow Sour Cream Sauce

12	marshmallows	12
1¼ cups	sour cream	300 mL
½ tsp.	vanilla (optional) OR 1 tbsp. (15 mL) orange-flavored liqueur	2 mL
	food coloring (optional)	

Place marshmallows in a small dish. Completely cover with sour cream. Cover and refrigerate overnight. If you wish, add the vanilla and food coloring. Beat until no lumps remain. Use as a sauce to spoon over fruit or as a dip for fruit.

Yield: 2 cups (500 mL).

See photograph on page 16A.

Citrus Sauce

1 cup	sour cream OR yogurt	250 mL
¼ cup	brown sugar	50 mL
1	orange, lemon or lime, grated peel	1
	icing sugar and orange slices for garnish	

Combine first 3 ingredients. Serve with French Toast sprinkled with icing sugar and then garnish with orange slices. Also a treat with pancakes or fresh fruit.

Caper Sauce

½ cup	mayonnaise	125 mL
½ cup	sour cream	125 mL
¼ cup	drained capers, chopped	50 mL
4 tbsp.	chopped green onion	60 mL
2 tbsp.	chopped OR slivered toasted almonds	30 mL
dash	pepper	dash

Thoroughly combine all the ingredients. Refrigerate. Serve cold or warm (do not boil when heating) over fish or vegetables.

Yield: 1-1½ cups (250-375 mL).

Russian Dressing

Homemade dressings are easy to make and a pleasure to serve.

½ cup	plain yogurt	125 mL
1 tbsp.	finely chopped onion	15 mL
1	red pepper, seeded and finely chopped	1
2 tbsp.	chili sauce OR seafood sauce	30 mL
1 tbsp.	ketchup	15 mL
1 tbsp.	prepared horseradish	15 mL
dash	lemon juice	dash
dash	garlic powder	dash
	brown sugar to taste	

Blend all ingredients together in a blender or food processor. Refrigerate at least 2 hours before serving.

Yield: 1 cup (250 mL).

Soups, Salads & Vegetables

Broccoli Buttermilk Soup

This is an excellent way to eat a nutritious vegetable that some people might otherwise find difficult to chew or digest. For a less spicy soup, decrease the peppers. We like it hot!

2	medium-large broccoli stalks, approximately 1 lb. (500 g)	2
2 cups	vegetable OR beef stock	500 mL
1	medium onion, quartered	1
1	bay leaf	1
1 tsp.	sweet basil	5 mL
½ tsp.	sugar	2 mL
1-2	garlic cloves	1-2
1¾ cups	buttermilk	425 mL
1/8 tsp.	black pepper	0.5 mL
1/8 tsp.	nutmeg	0.5 mL
pinch	cayenne pepper	pinch
	salt to taste (optional)	
	tomato slices for garnish (optional)	

Peel and slice the broccoli stalks. Cut or break the tops into florets. Place the broccoli, stock, onion, bay leaf, basil, sugar and garlic into a large pot. Bring the contents to a boil and then reduce the heat and cook until the broccoli is tender. Take the bay leaf out and discard. Process the broccoli mixture in a food processor or blender, a little at a time, until it is smooth. Return the mixture to the pot and gradually beat in the buttermilk with a whisk. Heat thoroughly, but do not boil. Add the pepper, nutmeg and cayenne. When serving, add a fresh slice of tomato to the center of the bowl. Also delicious served cold.

Serves: 4-6.

Faichuk Family Borsch

Made from fresh garden vegetables, this borsch is a truly delicious soup.

6-8	medium beets	6-8
10 cups	cold water (add extra water if necessary)	2.5 L
3 tbsp.	butter	45 mL
1	large onion, diced	1
¼ cup	reconstituted lemon juice	50 mL
3-4	carrots, diced	3-4
1 cup	fresh green OR yellow beans, cut diagonally in 2-3" (5-7.5 cm) pieces	250 mL
1 cup	diced new potatoes	250 mL
1 cup	diced celery (optional)	250 mL
2 tbsp.	flour	30 mL
½ cup	cold water	125 mL
2 tbsp.	chopped fresh dill	30 mL
	salt to taste	
1 cup	sour cream	250 mL

Wash beets thoroughly. Peel beets and then cut into fine strips. Place the beets in a large pot, along with the water, and simmer for 20 minutes. In the meantime, sauté the onion in the butter until soft. Add lemon juice, carrots, beans, potatoes, onions and celery, if using, to the beets. Simmer. Blend the flour and the ½ cup (125 mL) of water to a smooth paste. Stir into the vegetables. Add dill and salt. Bring to a boil. Simmer until the vegetables are tender. Add a dollop of sour cream to each bowl before serving or pass the sour cream at the table.

Variation: Just before serving, stir ½ cup (125 mL) soup into the sour cream. Then add to the soup. Do not boil. Warm and serve.

Serves: 8-10.

Stewed Tomato Soup

Excellent on a cold wintery day. Served with mashed potatoes and sausages — this is a family favorite.

19 oz.	can tomatoes (OR larger)	540 mL
2 tbsp.	brown sugar	30 mL
	pepper to taste	
dash	garlic powder (optional)	dash
2-3 tbsp.	plain yogurt	30-45 mL
	parsley sprigs to garnish	

Place the tomatoes in a saucepan (not aluminum). Mash or cut up the larger pieces of tomato and heat thoroughly on low-medium heat. Add the brown sugar, pepper and garlic. Stir thoroughly. Ladle piping hot into bowls, add yogurt to the center of each bowl and garnish with the parsley.

Serves: 3-4.

Cucumber Buttermilk Soup

A cool summer treat.

1½-2 cups	grated cucumber (peeled, seeded)	375-500 mL
4 cups	buttermilk	1 L
½ tsp.	salt OR to taste	2 mL
	pepper to taste	
¼ cup	snipped parsley	50 mL
1-2 tbsp.	minced green onion	15-30 mL
1	garlic clove, minced (optional)	1

Cucumber Buttermilk Soup (Cont'd.)

Combine all of the ingredients thoroughly. Chill, covered, for several hours. Stir before serving. Garnish with parsley sprigs or snipped onion greens.

As a variation, process all the ingredients in a blender until smooth. Chill and serve.

Serves: 8-10.

Hot Buttermilk Soup

½ cup	rice flour	125 mL
4 cups	buttermilk	1 L
½ cup	raisins OR canned fruit, drained	125 mL
1 tsp.	vanilla extract OR lemon peel	5 mL
½ cup	sugar	125 mL

In a pot, blend the buttermilk slowly into the flour. Put the pot on the burner at medium heat. Bring to a boil, beating constantly. Reduce the heat and cook for another 5 minutes. Add the raisins, flavoring, if desired, and sugar. Blend thoroughly. Serve warm. (If too thick, thin with buttermilk.) Also tasty as a sauce on Yogurt Cake (see recipe, page 106) or Ice Cream (see recipe, page 123).

Serves: 6-8.

Cold Buttermilk Soup

Danish in origin, this soup is refreshing on a hot summer day.

2	egg yolks	2
½ cup	honey OR sugar	125 mL
½ tsp.	grated lime rind (optional)	2 mL
1 tsp.	lime juice (optional)	5 mL
1 tsp.	almond extract	5 mL
4 cups	buttermilk	1 L

Topping

2	egg whites	2
1 tsp.	vinegar	5 mL
1 tsp.	sugar	5 mL
	fresh strawberries for garnish (optional)	

Beat the egg yolks in a large bowl. Slowly add honey, beating until the eggs fall back into the bowl in a ribbon when the beater is lifted. Add the lime rind, juice and almond extract if desired. Slowly beat in the buttermilk and continue to beat until the soup is smooth. Refrigerate. Stir before serving in chilled bowls. Prepare the topping by beating together the egg whites, vinegar and sugar. Just before serving, float the topping (like clouds) on the soup in each bowl. Garnish with sliced fresh strawberries for a beautiful treat.

Note: Leftover buttermilk soup makes a delicious base for Rice Pudding.

Serves: 6-8.

See photograph on front cover.

Tzatsiki

A Middle Eastern appetizer, salad or delicious cold tangy soup.

1	medium cucumber, peeled and grated	1
1 tsp.	salt OR to taste	5 mL
2-3 cups	plain yogurt	500-750 mL
2-3	cloves garlic, minced	2-3
1 tbsp.	olive oil	15 mL
1 tbsp.	fresh lemon juice	15 mL
2 tbsp.	chopped fresh mint OR dill	30 mL
	pita bread (optional)	

Appetizer

Sprinkle grated cucumber with salt and allow to stand for 1 hour. Drain off the resulting liquid. Squeeze the cucumber to release as much liquid as possible. Combine the cucumber, yogurt, garlic, olive oil and lemon juice. Cover and refrigerate for 8 hours or overnight. Stir before serving. Place in a 3-cup (750 mL) bowl and garnish with chopped mint or dill. Serve with pita triangles for dipping.

Serves: 6-10.

Salad

Serve on individual plates on a bed of lettuce. Garnish with fresh parsley sprigs (to freshen the breath). Serve with crusty rolls, lemonade or cold beer and sun-warmed peaches.

Serves: 4-6.

Soup

Do not drain the cucumber. Combine all the ingredients except for the mint or dill. Use 3 cups (750 mL) yogurt. You may want to increase the salt and lemon juice. Refrigerate, covered, overnight. Stir in chopped mint or dill before serving and garnish each bowl with a sprig of either mint or dill.

Serves: 4-6.

Blueberry Soup

We often enjoy stewed fruits (such as strawberries and rhubarb) for breakfast with toast or as a sweet-tart dessert instead of plain fruit. This blueberry soup, Swedish in origin, is an elegant treat for breakfast or as a dessert soup, or a cool beginning to a summer luncheon.

2 cups	water	500 mL
2½ cups	unsweetened pineapple juice	625 mL
¼ cup	sugar	50 mL
2	cinnamon sticks, halved	2
⅓ cup	lemon juice	75 mL
2 cups	blueberries	500 mL
3½-4 tbsp.	quick-cooking tapioca*	50-60 mL
¾ cup	lingonberries in sauce OR currant jelly	175 mL
1 cup	yogurt OR sour cream	250 mL
	mint sprigs for garnish (optional)	

In a large pot (not aluminum), combine water, pineapple juice, sugar, cinnamon sticks, lemon juice, blueberries and tapioca. Bring to a boil over medium heat; stirring gently. Reduce the heat and simmer, stirring as needed for about 3-5 minutes. Remove from the heat and stir in the lingonberries or currant jelly. Cool. Cover and refrigerate. Remove the cinnamon sticks. Serve cold with spoonfuls of yogurt or sour cream, garnished with a sprig of mint, in each bowl. Such a stunning presentation!

Serves: 6-8.

*Note: 2½-3 tbsp. (32-45 mL) cornstarch may be used in place of tapioca to thicken.

See photograph on page 48A.

Orange Medley Salad

1	head romaine lettuce	1
1	handful spinach leaves	1
¼-½ cup	fresh parsley	50-125 mL
10 oz	can mandarin orange sections, drained (reserve juice)	284 mL
1	small red onion, cut in rings	1
4	large mushrooms, sliced (optional)	4
¼ cup	pecans	50 mL
1/8 cup	raisins	25 mL

Remove the tough stems from the lettuce and spinach. Tear the lettuce, spinach and parsley into bite-size pieces. Add the remaining ingredients and toss together. Serve with Orange Yogurt Dressing, below.

Serves: 4-6.

Orange Yogurt Dressing

¼ cup	reserved orange juice	50 mL
½ cup	chopped cucumber	125 mL
1 tsp.	prepared horseradish	5 mL
1½ tsp.	chopped onion	7 mL
1 cup	plain yogurt	250 mL

Blend all ingredients in a blender or food processor until smooth. Chill for several hours before serving.

Yield: 1½ cups (375 mL).

Peach Nut Salad

1	head romaine lettuce	1
3	fresh peaches, sliced OR 14 oz. (398 mL) can peach slices, drained (reserve juice)	3
1	large avocado, peeled and sliced in wedges	1
1 tbsp.	lemon juice	1 tbsp.
½ cup	pecan halves OR sliced almonds	125 mL
⅓ cup	sour cream OR yogurt	75 mL
⅓ cup	mayonnaise	75 mL
1-2 tbsp.	peach juice	15-30 mL

On individual salad plates, place a bed of lettuce leaves. Arrange peach slices on each of the plates. Place the avocado wedges decoratively on top of the lettuce. Sprinkle the avocado with the lemon juice. Arrange the pecans on top of the peaches and avocado. In a small bowl, combine the sour cream, mayonnaise and peach juice until smooth. Drizzle over the salads.

Serves: 4-6.

For a refreshing drink blend (in a blender) 1 cup buttermilk and 1 cup Tomato Vegetable Drink. Pour into 2 glasses and garnish with lemon slices.

Mix equal parts of cold yogurt and cold fruit juice for a creamy drink.

Layered Salad

A colorful and tasty salad that you make a day ahead.

1	head lettuce, torn in bite-size pieces	1
1½ cups	chopped celery	375 mL
1	green OR red pepper, chopped	1
1	onion, finely sliced	1
10 oz.	pkg. frozen peas	283 g
1 cup	mayonnaise	250 mL
½ cup	plain yogurt	125 mL
½ cup	sour cream	125 mL
2 tbsp.	sugar	30 mL
¾ tsp.	basil	3 mL
1½ cups	grated Cheddar cheese	375 mL
9	strips bacon, cooked and crumbled	9
¼ cup	chopped fresh mushrooms	50 mL

In a 9 x 13" (22 x 33 cm) glass pan, or a favorite glass salad bowl, layer the lettuce, celery, pepper, onion and peas. Combine the mayonnaise, yogurt, sour cream, sugar and basil. Spread over the other ingredients. Top with the cheese and bacon. Cover with plastic wrap and refrigerate for 24 hours. Just before serving, sprinkle the mushrooms over the salad.

Serves: 10-12.

Spinach Salad With Buttermilk Dressing

Prepare dressing a few hours ahead to allow the flavors to blend.

½ lb.	fresh spinach	250 g
8 oz.	can sliced water chestnuts, drained	250 mL
2	green onions, sliced	2
6	large mushrooms, sliced	6
1 cup	croutons	250 mL

Tear the spinach in bite-size pieces. Gently toss the spinach, along with the water chestnuts, onions, mushrooms and croutons. Serve with the following dressing.

Dressing

⅔ cup	mayonnaise	150 mL
½ cup	buttermilk	125 mL
2 tsp.	parsley flakes	10 mL
1/8 tsp.	teryaki sauce	0.5 mL
2	garlic cloves, minced	2
dash	pepper	dash

Prepare dressing by combining the mayonnaise, buttermilk, parsley, teryaki sauce, garlic and pepper in a small bowl. Blend well and refrigerate for several hours.

Serves: 6.

See photograph on page 80A.

Coleslaw

A colorful addition to any meal.

5 cups	shredded green cabbage	1.25 L
½	green pepper, diced	½
½	red pepper, diced	½
2	carrots, grated	2
3	green onions, thinly sliced	3
½ cup	finely chopped celery (optional)	125 mL
¾ cup	mayonnaise	175 mL
¼ cup	sour cream	50 mL
1 tbsp.	apple cider vinegar	15 mL
1 tsp.	celery salt	5 mL
	pepper to taste	

In a large bowl, toss together the cabbage, peppers, carrots, onions and celery. Combine the mayonnaise, sour cream, vinegar, celery salt and pepper. Add to vegetables and toss to coat. Cover and chill.

Serves: 8-10.

Variation: Fruited coleslaw is a refreshing treat. Substitute 1 tsp. (5 mL) sugar for celery salt in above dressing and pour dressing over 2 cups (500 mL) crushed cabbage, ½ cup (125 mL) drained crushed pineapple (add juice to dressing) and 2 tart apples, diced.

Apple cider vinegar is a natural diuretic.

Cucumbers In Sour Cream

A cool salad often found at Nova Scotia gatherings.

3-4	cucumbers, peeled and thinly sliced	3-4
2 tbsp.	salt	30 mL
½ tsp.	black pepper	2 mL
2 tbsp.	sugar	30 mL
2 tbsp.	vinegar	30 mL
1-1½ cups	sour cream	250-375 mL
	parsley sprigs for garnish (optional)	

Place cucumbers in a bowl. Sprinkle with salt, cover with a plate and let stand for 3 hours. Rinse the cucumbers in cold water and then squeeze out the moisture. Combine the remaining ingredients, then add the cucumbers and blend thoroughly. Refrigerate. At serving time, garnish with parsley.

Serves: 6-10.

When using dried herbs, crush or roll them with your fingers before adding to the recipe. Crushing brings out the natural flavors.

Wash and dry parsley, then refrigerate in a covered container to maintain freshness and crispness.

Potato Salad

A must for every summer picnic.

½ cup	plain yogurt	125 mL
½ cup	mayonnaise	125 mL
2 tsp.	prepared mustard	10 mL
1 tsp.	curry powder (optional)	5 mL
2 cups	cooked and cubed potatoes	500 mL
1 cup	peeled and diced cucumber	250 mL
½ cup	chopped celery	125 mL
¼ cup	chopped green onion	50 mL
	salt and pepper to taste	
	parsley sprigs and tomato wedges for garnish	

In a large bowl, combine the yogurt, mayonnaise, mustard and curry. Add remaining ingredients; toss to mix well. Refrigerate for a few hours to blend flavors. Garnish with fresh parsley and tomato wedges.

Serves: 6-8.

Immediately refrigerate leftovers or foods cooked for later use. Do not allow the foods to sit at room temperature. Harmful bacteria can be produced.

Potatoes contain no fat or cholesterol.

Asparagus Spears With Tomato Sauce

Maintain the delicate asparagus flavor by not overcooking.

1 lb.	asparagus	500 g
¼ cup	sour cream OR yogurt	50 mL
¼ cup	mayonnaise	50 mL
¼ tsp.	salt	1 mL
	pepper to taste	
1	medium tomato, peeled and diced	1
1	large tomato	1
	lemon juice	
	tomato wedges and sweet basil for garnish	

Snap or cut off the woody base of the asparagus stalks. Cook, uncovered, in a small amount of salted water for approximately 10 minutes — just until tender. Drain and chill or serve warm. Combine the sour cream, mayonnaise, salt and pepper and diced tomato. Cut a slice off the top of the large tomato and scoop out the pulp. Spoon half the dressing into the tomato shell; place the tomato in the center of a serving platter. Arrange the chilled asparagus, in bundles of 3 or 4 stalks, around the tomato. Sprinkle the lemon juice over the asparagus. Drizzle the bundles with the remaining dressing. Garnish with tomato wedges and basil.

Serves: 4-6.

See photograph on page 80A.

Oriental Shrimp Salad

2 cups	cooked small OR large shrimp, fresh OR canned	500 mL
1 cup	finely chopped celery	250 mL
¼-½ cup	pineapple chunks	50-125 mL
6-8	cherry tomatoes, quartered lengthwise	6-8
¼ cup	each chopped red and green pepper	50 mL
8 oz.	can water chestnuts, drained and chopped	227 mL
2	green onions, chopped	2
¼ cup	sour cream	50 mL
¼ cup	mayonnaise	50 mL
1 tbsp.	soy sauce	15 mL
1 tsp.	lemon juice	5 mL
dash	paprika for garnish	dash

In a large bowl, combine shrimp, celery, pineapple, tomatoes, peppers, water chestnuts and onions. In a small bowl, combine the sour cream, mayonnaise, soy sauce and lemon juice. Cover both mixtures; refrigerate for several hours to blend flavors. At serving time, lightly loss shrimp mixture with sour cream mixture. Serve on a bed of lettuce. Garnish with paprika.

Serves: 4.

Croutons are easy to make. Cut stale or fresh bread into cubes. Put them on a cookie sheet and sprinkle with garlic powder, onion salt or grated Parmesan cheese. Bake in a 275°F (140°C) oven for approximately 30 minutes. Turn off the oven and leave ½-1 hour until the cubes are crisp. Enjoy on your favorite salad.

Seafood Salad

A maritime treat!

4 oz.	can lobster meat, drained	113 g
4 oz.	can crab meat, drained	113 g
1 cup	chopped celery	250 mL
14 oz.	can pineapple chunks, well drained	398 mL
½ cup	plain yogurt	125 mL
1½ tsp.	Worcestershire sauce	7 mL
2 tbsp.	lemon juice	30 mL
	salt and pepper to taste	
1 tbsp.	minced onion (optional)	15 mL
¼ cup	sliced, pitted ripe olives (optional)	50 mL
	parsley sprigs and lemon twists for garnish	

In a large bowl, flake the lobster and crab. Add the celery, pineapple, yogurt, Worcestershire sauce, lemon juice, salt, pepper, onion and olives, if desired. Toss thoroughly and refrigerate for at least 1 hour. To serve, arrange on a plate lined with a bed of lettuce. Garnish with parsley and lemon twists.

Serves: 4.

Turkey Medley Salad

1½ cups	diced cooked turkey	375 mL
½	pkg. fresh spinach, washed, dried and torn into bite-size pieces	½
2	stalks celery, diagonally sliced	2
10 oz.	can mandarin orange sections, drained	284 mL
½ cup	slivered OR broken cashew nuts	125 mL

Dressing

½ cup	yogurt	125 mL
2 tbsp.	lemon juice	30 mL
1 tsp.	dry mustard	5 mL
	salt and pepper to taste	

In a large bowl, combine the turkey, spinach, celery and orange sections. In another bowl, combine the yogurt, lemon juice, mustard and salt and pepper. Pour the dressing over the salad and toss gently to coat. Garnish with cashew nuts.

Serves: 4.

Slice submarine buns 3/4 of the way through. Remove a small amount of the bread from the center, top and bottom. Fill the bun with your favorite filling, close and wrap in plastic wrap. Refrigerate until well chilled. Slice the loaf in 1/2" (1.3 cm) slices and arrange on a fancy sandwich tray.

Cantaloupe Stuffed with Turkey

Colorful, with a gourmet appearance, yet easy to prepare. The walnuts add a pleasant texture contrast.

2	small cantaloupes	2
1 tsp.	lemon juice	5 mL
⅓ cup	plain yogurt	75 mL
¼ cup	mayonnaise	50 mL
2 tbsp.	finely chopped mango chutney	30 mL
1 tsp.	brown sugar (optional)	5 mL
2 cups	diced cooked turkey OR chicken	500 mL
¾ cup	seedless grapes, halved, reserve a few for garnish	175 mL
	salt to taste	
¼ cup	walnuts	50 mL

Using a saw-tooth pattern, cut the cantaloupes in 2 and remove the pulp. Remove several melon balls from each half to use as garnish. Sprinkle the balls with the lemon juice to prevent browning. In a small bowl, mix the yogurt, mayonnaise, chutney and brown sugar. Combine the turkey and grapes; then blend in the salt and the yogurt mixture. Stuff each melon half with the turkey mixture, top with melon balls and walnuts.

Serves: 4.

See photograph on page 48A.

Fancy Green Beans

3 cups	fresh OR frozen French-style green beans (amount to serve 4)	750 mL
1-2 tbsp.	sour cream	15-30 mL
	salt and pepper to taste	
	garlic powder and oregano to taste	
¼ cup	slivered plain OR toasted almonds	50 mL

Cook beans to tender-crisp. Mix sour cream, salt and pepper, several shakes of garlic powder and oregano and the almonds. Drain beans and toss with sour cream mixture. Serve immediately.

Serves: 4.

See photograph on back cover.

Broccoli With Yogurt Sauce

3 cups	broccoli florets, steamed tender-crisp	750 mL
2 cups	plain yogurt	500 mL
2 tsp.	flour	30 mL
½ tsp.	pepper	2 mL
1	garlic clove, minced	1
½ tsp.	Worcestershire sauce	2 mL
1 tbsp.	lemon juice	15 mL
1 cup	shredded Cheddar cheese	250 mL

Place the broccoli in a buttered casserole. Combine in a separate bowl, the yogurt, flour, pepper, garlic, Worcestershire sauce and lemon juice. Fold in the cheese. Pour over the broccoli. Bake at 350°F (180°C) for approximately 20-25 minutes or until thoroughly heated.

Serves: 4-6.

Teryaki Mushrooms In Sour Cream

A creamy blend of flavors that adds delightfully to any menu. These mushrooms go well with Herbed Yogurt Rice, page 50.

4 tbsp.	butter	60 mL
1	medium onion, chopped	1
1 lb.	fresh mushrooms, sliced	500 g
1-2 tbsp.	teryaki sauce	15-30 mL
½ cup	sour cream OR plain yogurt	125 mL
3 tbsp.	freshly chopped parsley	45 mL

Melt the butter in a frying pan over medium heat. Add onion and cook until transparent. Add the mushrooms and cook, stirring occasionally until soft. Pour in teryaki sauce and stir. Add the sour cream to the mushroom-onion mixture and thoroughly warm, stirring frequently. Do NOT boil. Stir in the parsley and serve with your favorite fish, poultry or meat.

Serves: 4-6.

See photograph on back cover.

A dash of cayenne pepper added to a hot lemon drink in the evening will help you stay warmer.

Carrots and Cauliflower

A colorful and nutritious combination.

1	cauliflower, broken OR cut in florets	1
4	carrots, diagonally sliced	4
1-2	green onions, finely chopped	1-2
1 tsp.	olive oil	5 mL
4 tbsp.	apple cider vinegar	60 mL
1 tbsp.	soy sauce	15 mL
¼ cup	sour cream	50 mL
dash	garlic powder	dash
	pepper to taste	
dash	celery salt	dash
	freshly ground pepper and parsley sprigs for garnish	

Steam or microwave the cauliflower and carrots until tender-crisp. Combine the onions, olive oil, cider vinegar, soy sauce, sour cream, garlic, pepper and celery salt. Mix thoroughly. Pour over drained, hot vegetables. Serve hot or refrigerate and serve cold. Toss before serving. Garnish with freshly ground pepper and parsley sprigs.

Serves: 4-6.

Creamy Onions Au Gratin

A scrumptious addition to a roast beef or roast pork dinner. Super for buffet entertaining.

4 cups	sliced onions, ½" (1.3 cm) thick	1 L
½ tsp.	salt	2 mL
1 cup	boiling water (retain liquid after cooking)	250 mL

Sauce

2 tbsp.	butter OR margarine	30 mL
2 tbsp.	flour	30 mL
	salt (optional)	
	pepper to taste	
1 cup	sour cream OR plain yogurt	250 mL
¾ cup	onion liquid	175 mL
¾ cup	grated Cheddar cheese	175 mL
½ cup	bread crumbs	125 mL
1-2 tbsp.	soft butter	15-30 mL

Cook the sliced onions in the salted boiling water for 10 minutes. Drain. Retain ¾ cup (175 mL) liquid for sauce. Place the onions in a buttered baking dish. In the original pot, melt the 2 tbsp. (30 mL) butter, stir in the flour to make a smooth paste. Remove from heat. Add the salt, pepper, sour cream, onion liquid and cheese. Stir until smooth and cheese is melted. Pour sauce over the onions. Combine bread crumbs and soft butter. Spread over the sauce. Cover and bake at 375°F (190°C) for 25-30 minutes.

Serves: 6.

Note: If a thinner sauce is desired, increase the boiling water to 1½-1¾ cups (375-425 mL), which in turn will increase onion liquid.

Blueberry Soup, page 32
Drop Scones, page 58
Johnny Cake Muffins, page 56
Frosty Banana Yogurt, page 123
Cantaloupe Stuffed With Turkey, page 44

Pan-Fried Baked Potatoes

¼ cup	butter	50 mL
¼ cup	vegetable oil	50 mL
6-7	large, cold, baked potatoes, peeled, sliced in ½" (1.3 cm) rounds	6-7
4	green onions, finely chopped	4
1 tsp.	dill weed	5 mL
	salt and pepper to taste	
1 cup	sour cream OR plain yogurt	250 mL
½ tsp.	dill weed	2 mL
	dill sprigs for garnish (optional)	

Heat butter and oil in large skillet over medium-high heat. Add potatoes and cook until golden, turning gently. Add onions and 1 tsp. (5 mL) dill weed and cook for another few minutes. Season to taste with salt and pepper. Remove to a platter with a slotted spoon and fork. Blot gently with a paper towel to remove excess oil. Mix sour cream or yogurt with ½ tsp. (2 mL) dill weed and spoon dollops of this over potatoes. Garnish with dill sprigs.

Serves: 4-6.

Creamy Cheesy Potatoes

Excellent for company and buffets.

5 lbs.	potatoes	2.5 kg
8 oz.	cream cheese	250 g
1 cup	sour cream	250 mL
2 tsp.	onion salt	10 mL
1 tsp.	pepper	5 mL
	butter	

Creamy Potatoes (Cont'd.)

Cook potatoes until tender in boiling water. Drain and mash the potatoes, then add the cream cheese, sour cream, onion salt and pepper. Beat well until creamy smooth. Place in a buttered casserole and bake at 350°F (180°C) for 30 minutes. Dot with butter before serving.

Serves: 10-12.

Herbed Yogurt Rice

Yogurt can be folded into plain or wild rice before serving. This is an especially tasty rice dish.

3 tbsp.	butter	45 mL
1	small onion, chopped	1
1 cup	rice	250mL
2 cups	hot chicken OR vegetable stock	500 mL
3 tbsp.	chopped fresh mint OR 1 tbsp. (15 mL) dried mint	45 mL
3 tbsp.	parsley flakes	45 mL
dash	pepper	dash
½ cup	plain yogurt	125 mL

Melt butter in a large skillet. Add onion and sauté until transparent. Add the rice and sauté for approximately 5 additional minutes, until the rice is golden brown. (Do NOT burn.) Add the hot stock and bring to a boil. Cover and cook on low heat for 15-20 minutes. Remove from the heat and stir in the mint, parsley, pepper and yogurt. Mix well; cover and let stand for 5 minutes. Serve with salmon steak.

Serves: 4-6.

See photograph on back cover.

Muffins, Breads & Pancakes

Refrigerator Raisin Bran Muffins

So good and so convenient to have the batter on hand in the refrigerator.

2 cups	boiling water	500 mL
2 cups	"all-bran" cereal	500 mL
3 cups	white sugar	750 mL
1 cup	shortening	250 mL
4	eggs	4
4 cups	buttermilk	1 L
3 tbsp.	baking soda	45 mL
1 tbsp.	salt	15 mL
5 cups	all-purpose flour	1.25 L
4 cups	bran flakes	1 L
2 cups	raisins	500 mL

Pour boiling water over the "all-bran"; let stand. Cream sugar, shortening and eggs. Add buttermilk, then the "all-bran" mixture. Add dry ingredients, except for the bran flakes, and mix well. Fold in bran flakes and raisins. Do not bake the first day. Bake at 400°F (200°C) for 15-20 minutes. Batter can be refrigerated for several weeks.

Yield: 4-5 dozen.

Variation: Try replacing with the following ingredients to produce a less sweet muffin: 2¼ cups (550 mL) boiling water, 3 cups (750 mL) "all-bran", 2 cups (500 mL) sugar, little or no salt, 4 cups (1 L) white and 1 cup (250 mL) whole-wheat flour. Other ingredients remain the same.

Apple-Bran Muffins

The apple/raisin combination makes a moist and tasty addition to the bran that is so good for you.

1 cup	sour cream OR yogurt	250 mL
½ cup	vegetable oil OR shortening	125 mL
1	egg	1
1 tsp.	vanilla	5 mL
1 cup	flour	250 mL
1 cup	natural bran	250 mL
½-1 cup	brown sugar	125-250 mL
1 tsp.	baking soda	5 mL
1	apple, peeled and diced	1
¾ cup	raisins	175 mL
½ tsp.	cinnamon (optional)	2 mL

Mix together the sour cream, oil, egg and vanilla. In a large bowl, combine the flour, bran, sugar and soda. Make a well in the dry ingredients and pour in the liquid mixture. Add the apple, raisins and cinnamon. Mix until just combined. Spoon into 12 greased muffin tins. Bake at 350°F (180°C) for 25-30 minutes.

Yield: 12.

Giant Blueberry Muffins

Light, not too sweet and packed with berries.

2	large eggs	2
⅔ cup	white sugar OR less	150 mL
½ cup	melted butter	125 mL
2 cups	buttermilk	500 mL
3 cups	all-purpose flour OR half white flour and half whole-wheat flour	750 mL
2 tbsp.	baking powder	30 mL
¼ tsp.	salt	1 mL
1 tsp.	vanilla	5 mL
3 cups	fresh OR frozen blueberries, well-drained	750 mL

Preheat oven to 400°F (200°C). In a bowl, beat eggs, add sugar and butter and mix well. Stir in the buttermilk. Combine the flour, baking powder and salt and stir gently into egg mixture, just enough to form a lumpy batter. Do not overmix. Fold in vanilla and blueberries and spoon into greased muffin tins, filling them almost to the top. Bake for 20-25 minutes or until firm. Serve warm. These muffins freeze well.

Yield: 24.

Note: The blueberries need not be thawed. Dust the blueberries with flour before folding into the batter, if desired.

Blueberry-Oat Muffins

Rolled oats are a nutritious addition to any recipe. Combined with buttermilk and blueberries, they provide a healthy muffin for breakfast or lunchbox.

1 cup	rolled oats	250 mL
1 cup	buttermilk	250 mL
1 cup	all-purpose flour	250 mL
1 tsp.	baking powder	5 mL
½ tsp.	baking soda	2 mL
½ tsp.	salt	2 mL
¾ cup	lightly packed brown sugar	175 mL
1	egg, beaten	1
¼ cup	melted butter	50 mL
1 cup	fresh OR frozen blueberries, well-drained	250 mL

Combine the rolled oats and buttermilk in a small bowl. Let stand. Combine flour, baking powder, baking soda, salt and sugar in a mixing bowl. Stir well to blend. Add the egg and melted butter to the oat mixture. Mix well. Add oat mixture all at once to the dry ingredients. Stir just until the ingredients are moistened. Gently fold in blueberries. Fill well-greased muffins cups ¾ full. Bake at 400°F (200°C) for 15-20 minutes.

Yield: 12.

Banana-Pineapple Muffins

1 cup	sour cream	250 mL
1	egg, well-beaten	1
½ cup	sugar	125 mL
2 tbsp.	shortening	30 mL
2 cups	sifted all-purpose flour	500 mL
1 tsp.	baking powder	5 mL
½ tsp.	baking soda	2 mL
½-1 cup	mashed bananas	125-250 mL
½ cup	crushed pineapple, well drained	125 mL
1 tsp.	vanilla	5 mL
1 tsp.	nutmeg	5 mL

Blend sour cream, egg, sugar and shortening together, mixing well. Resift flour with baking powder and baking soda. Add to first mixture, stirring just until blended. Stir in banana, pineapple, vanilla and nutmeg. Spoon into greased, medium-size muffin pans. Bake in a 375-400°F (190-200°C) oven for 20-25 minutes. These muffins freeze well.

Yield: 12.

Johnny Cake Muffins

¾ cup	cornmeal	175 mL
1¼ cups	buttermilk	300 mL
1 cup	all-purpose flour	250 mL
1 tbsp.	baking powder	15 mL
⅓ cup	brown sugar	75 mL
1	egg, slightly beaten	1
¼ cup	melted shortening	50 mL
½ tsp.	vanilla	2 mL
1 tbsp.	grated orange peel (optional)	15 mL

Johnny Cake Muffins (Cont'd.)

Preheat oven to 400°F (200°C). Grease 12 muffins cups. Mix together the cornmeal and the buttermilk; set aside for 5 minutes. Sift together the flour and baking powder and then stir in the brown sugar. Stir the egg, shortening, vanilla and optional peel into the cornmeal mixture. Add the liquid ingredients to the dry. Stir until just combined. Fill the muffin tins approximately ⅔ full. Bake 20-25 minutes.

Yield: 12.

See photograph on page 48A.

Nutmeg Muffins

¼ cup	shortening	50 mL
1 cup	brown sugar	250 mL
1	egg, beaten	1
1 cup	buttermilk	250 mL
1½ cups	whole-wheat flour	375 mL
½ cup	all-purpose flour	125 mL
½ tsp.	baking powder	2 mL
1 tsp.	baking soda	5 mL
½ tsp.	salt	2 mL
1 tsp.	nutmeg (heaping)	5 mL
1 cup	raisins	250 mL

Cream shortening and sugar, add egg and buttermilk. In a separate bowl, combine dry ingredients. Stir creamed mixture into dry ingredients until just moistened. Fold in raisins. Spoon into greased muffin tins. Bake in 350°F (180°C) oven for 20 minutes, until golden brown.

Yield: 12.

Drop Scones

Delicious as is or with jam and/or Devonshire Cream.

1 cup	lard	250 mL
1 cup	sugar	250 mL
4 cups	all-purpose flour	1 L
1 tbsp.	baking powder	15 mL
1 tsp.	baking soda	5 mL
1 tsp.	salt (optional)	5 mL
1 cup	currants OR raisins	250 mL
2 cups	buttermilk	500 mL

Mix the first 6 ingredients together with a pastry blender or by hand. Add currants then buttermilk. Stir to moisten. Drop by tablespoons (15 mL) onto a greased cookie sheet. Bake in a 375°F (190°C) oven for about 15 minutes, or until golden brown.

Yield: 36 scones.

Variation: Brush with egg white and sprinkle with sugar before baking.

See photograph on page 48A.

Cheddar-Buttermilk Biscuits

2 cups	all-purpose flour	500 mL
2 tsp.	baking powder	10 mL
1 tsp.	baking soda	5 mL
⅓ cup	shortening	75 mL
¾ cup	grated Cheddar cheese	175 mL
1 cup	buttermilk	250 mL

Cheddar Biscuits (Cont'd.)

Combine flour, baking powder and baking soda; mix well. Cut in shortening until crumbly. Stir in grated cheese. Add buttermilk, stirring with a fork to make a soft, slightly sticky dough. Turn dough onto a lightly floured board and knead about 10 times. Roll out ½" (1.3 cm) thick and cut into 2½" (6.5 cm) rounds. Bake on an ungreased baking sheet at 425°F (220°C) for 10-12 minutes.

Yield: 12-14 biscuits.

Butterscotch Nut Bread

Nuts are an attractive, tasty addition to this loaf.

2 cups	all-purpose flour	500 mL
1 tsp.	baking powder	5 mL
½ tsp.	baking soda	2 mL
1 tsp.	salt	5 mL
1 cup	brown sugar	250 mL
½ cup	chopped walnuts OR pecans	125 mL
2	eggs, well-beaten	2
1 cup	buttermilk	250 mL
2 tsp.	melted butter	10 mL

Sift together the flour, baking powder, baking soda and salt. Add the sugar and nuts. Combine the eggs, buttermilk and butter and add to the dry ingredients. Mix just enough to moisten. Pour into a greased loaf pan and bake at 350°F (180°C) for 45-50 minutes. Store 1 day before serving for best flavor.

Yield: 1 loaf.

Ham 'n' Cheese Muffins

A meal in a muffin! Great for lunches and lunchbox.

2 cups	all-purpose flour	500 mL
½ cup	sugar	125 mL
1 tbsp.	baking powder	15 mL
1½ tsp.	baking soda	7 mL
1 cup	plain yogurt	250 mL
½ cup	melted butter	125 mL
2	eggs, beaten	2
1 cup	shredded mozzarella OR Cheddar cheese	250 mL
½-1 cup	chopped cooked ham	125-250 mL
1 tsp.	basil (measure, then rub into mixture)	5 mL

In a large bowl, stir together the flour, sugar, baking powder and baking soda. In a small bowl, thoroughly combine the yogurt, butter and eggs. Add all at once to dry ingredients; stir just until moistened. Quickly fold in the cheese, ham and basil. Divide batter evenly among 12 large, greased muffin cups. Bake at 400°F (200°C) for 18-20 minutes. Serve warm. Store in the refrigerator.

Yield: 12.

Place a piece of aluminum foil under the napkins in your bun or muffin basket to keep muffins warm longer.

Cinnamon Loaf

The cinnamon swirl makes this a very pretty loaf.

½ cup	shortening	125 mL
1 cup	white sugar	250 mL
2	eggs	2
2 cups	all-purpose flour	500 mL
½ tsp.	baking powder	2 mL
½ tsp.	baking soda	2 mL
½ tsp.	salt (optional)	2 mL
1 cup	buttermilk	250 mL
1 tbsp.	cinnamon	15 mL
1½ tbsp.	sugar	22 mL

Cream shortening, sugar and eggs. Sift together the dry ingredients and add, alternately with buttermilk to the shortening mixture. Mix the cinnamon with the sugar in a dish. Reserve a small amount to sprinkle on the top of the loaf. Pour the batter into a prepared loaf pan. Mix the cinnamon through the batter with a swirling motion. Sprinkle with remainder of the cinnamon mixture. Bake at 350°F (180°C) for 55-60 minutes.

Yield: 1 loaf.

Measure your ingredients before you start to bake, especially if you are halving or doubling a recipe. You will be less likely to make mistakes and more likely to be happy with the finished product.

Banana Bread

Almost everyone loves banana bread. Try some for breakfast for a change.

½ cup	butter OR margarine	125 mL
1 cup	white sugar	250 mL
2	eggs	2
1 tsp.	vanilla	5 mL
2-3	bananas, mashed	2-3
⅔ cup	buttermilk	150 mL
2 cups	all-purpose flour	500 mL
½ tsp.	baking soda	2 mL
2 tsp.	baking powder	10 mL
¼ tsp.	salt	1 mL
½ cup	chopped walnuts OR pecans (optional)	125 mL

Cream butter and sugar together. Add eggs and vanilla and blend well. Combine bananas and buttermilk. Sift all dry ingredients together. Add half of the dry ingredients along with the liquid mixture to the creamed mixture. Mix well, then add the remainder of the dry ingredients and blend. Stir in the nuts. Line the bottom of a greased loaf pan with wax paper. Pour batter into the pan and bake at 375°F (190°C) for 40-45 minutes or until a toothpick inserted in the center comes out clean.

Yield: 1 loaf.

Freeze ripe bananas in their skins. Peel and use directly from the freezer in blended yogurt treats or thaw and mash for use in your favorite banana recipes.

Zucchini Bread

1⅔ cups	all-purpose flour	400 mL
½ cup	firmly packed brown sugar	125 mL
¾ cup	white sugar	175 mL
1 tsp.	baking soda	5 mL
1 tsp.	cinnamon	5 mL
½ tsp.	salt	2 mL
¼ tsp.	nutmeg	1 mL
½ cup	buttermilk	125 mL
⅓ cup	vegetable oil	75 mL
2	eggs, slightly beaten	2
1 tbsp.	grated lemon peel	15 mL
1 tsp.	vanilla	5 mL
1½ cups	grated zucchini, well-drained	375 mL
1 cup	chopped walnuts (optional)	250 mL
	powdered sugar (optional)	

Combine flour, sugars, baking soda, cinnamon, salt and nutmeg in a large bowl and mix well. Combine buttermilk, oil, eggs, lemon peel and vanilla in another bowl and mix well. Add liquids to the dry ingredients. Stir until just moist. Stir in zucchini and nuts. Turn into a prepared loaf pan. Bake at 350°F (180°C) for 45-50 minutes or until a toothpick inserted in the center of the loaf comes out clean. Sprinkle lightly with powdered sugar.

Yield: 1 loaf.

Sour Cream Coffee Cake

So light and tasty, it's hard to resist a second piece.

1 cup	sour cream	250 mL
1 tsp.	baking soda	5 mL
½ cup	soft butter	125 mL
1 cup	sugar	250 mL
2	eggs, well-beaten	2
1 tsp.	vanilla	5 mL
1¾ cups	sifted cake flour	425 mL
2 tsp.	baking powder	10 mL

Topping

¼ cup	brown sugar	50 mL
1 tbsp.	cinnamon	15 mL
2 tbsp.	finely chopped pecans	30 mL

Grease and flour an 8" (20 cm) square cake pan. Preheat oven to 350°F (180°C). Combine sour cream and baking soda in a bowl and set aside. In a large mixing bowl, blend butter and sugar thoroughly. Add eggs and vanilla; beat well. Alternately add sifted dry ingredients and sour cream. In a small bowl, combine the topping ingredients. Spread half of the batter in the prepared pan. Sprinkle with half of the topping. Repeat with remaining batter and topping. Bake for 45-50 minutes. Serve warm.

Yield: 12 pieces.

Cranberries and cranberry juice are excellent sources of Vitamin C.

Cranberry Streusel Coffee Cake

As pleasant to look at as it is tasty. Try this delicious treat with blueberries or peach slices in place of cranberries.

Streusel

¾ cup	brown sugar	175 mL
1 tsp.	cinnamon	5 mL
¼ cup	butter	50 mL

Cake

½ cup	butter	125 mL
1 cup	sugar	250 mL
2	eggs	2
1 tsp.	vanilla	5 mL
2 tsp.	grated orange peel	10 mL
2 cups	flour	500 mL
1 tsp.	baking powder	5 mL
1 tsp.	baking soda	5 mL
1 cup	yogurt	250 mL
2 cups	cranberries	500 mL

Prepare streusel by mixing brown sugar and cinnamon together; then cut in butter until crumbly. Set aside. Prepare cake by creaming together the butter and sugar until fluffy. Add eggs, vanilla and orange peel. Add dry ingredients alternately with yogurt. Spread half the batter in a greased and floured 9" or 10" (23 or 25 cm) springform pan. Sprinkle with all the berries and half the streusel. Add remaining batter. Sprinkle with remaining streusel. Bake for 1 hour at 350°F (180°C).

Serves: 10-12.

Quick Spice Buns

2 cups	all-purpose flour	500 mL
½ tsp.	baking soda	2 mL
½ tsp.	salt	2 mL
2 tbsp.	sugar	30 mL
¾ cup	buttermilk	175 mL
	softened butter	
¼-½ cup	brown sugar	50-125 mL
1 tsp.	cinnamon	5 mL
½ tsp.	nutmeg	2 mL
¼ tsp.	cloves	1 mL

Sift together flour, baking soda, salt and sugar, until the flour is granular in texture. Add buttermilk to make a stiff dough. Knead lightly on a floured board. Roll to ¼" (.5 cm) thickness to form a rectangle. Spread with softened butter and sprinkle with the brown sugar and spices. Roll up like a jelly roll and cut in ¾" (1.9 cm) slices. Place on a buttered baking sheet, cut side down. Bake 15-20 minutes in a 450°F (230°C) oven. Serve as is or ice with Butter Icing.

Yield: 12.

Butter Icing

3 tbsp.	butter	45 mL
2 tbsp.	buttermilk OR milk	30 mL
1 tsp.	vanilla extract	5 mL
2-2¼ cups	sifted icing sugar	500-550 mL

Cream butter. Add milk, vanilla and a little of the icing sugar. Mix well. Gradually add remaining icing sugar, while mixing, until it reaches good spreading consistency. Icing should hold its shape.

Yield: Approximately 2 cups (500 mL).

Apple-Cinnamon Yogurt Pancakes

Provides a thin, light, crêpe-like pancake. The apple gives an intriguing taste and texture contrast.

1 cup	sifted all-purpose flour	250 mL
1 tbsp.	sugar	15 mL
¾ tsp.	baking soda	3 mL
½ tsp.	salt	2 mL
4	eggs	4
1 cup	plain yogurt	250 mL
¼ cup	water	50 mL
2 tbsp.	melted butter	30 mL
1	medium apple, peeled and diced	1
1-1½ tsp.	cinnamon	5-7 mL

Sift flour, sugar, baking soda and salt together. Beat eggs until light, blend in yogurt and water. Stir in melted butter. Stir in apple and cinnamon. Add dry ingredients and blend. Cook on a lightly oiled, hot griddle.

Yield: 16 medium-size pancakes.

Try dabbing yogurt on crêpes, instead of whipping cream.

Light and Fluffy Buttermilk Pancakes

These are great for Saturday breakfast or brunch. We make all three varieties with one batter, to accommodate all the family tastes.

2 cups	sifted all-purpose flour	500 mL
½ tsp.	salt (optional)	2 mL
1 tsp.	baking soda	5 mL
2	eggs, well beaten	2
2 cups	buttermilk	500 mL
¼ cup	sunflower oil	50 mL
2 tbsp.	sugar (optional)	30 mL

Sift together the flour, salt and baking soda. Stir in the eggs and buttermilk (batter will be somewhat lumpy). Fold in the oil and sugar, if desired. Cook on a buttered, hot griddle. Cook until tiny bubbles appear and break on the surface; turn and brown the other side. Extra butter may be required on the griddle between pancakes. Serve warm, as is, or with syrup, raspberry or strawberry jam.

Yield: 16 medium-size pancakes.

Variations:

Blueberry Pancakes

Add ½ cup (125 mL) fresh or frozen blueberries, lightly dusted with flour, to the above batter. Pancakes will take a little longer to cook. Watch when eating — the blueberries are hot!

Buttermilk (or Blueberry) Pancakes with Bacon

Reminiscent of pancakes served at Calgary Stampede Breakfasts!

Precook bacon to your liking. Drain and pat excess grease from bacon with paper towels. Cut each piece in half. Place 1 or 2 halves on the griddle for each pancake. Pour pancake batter over the bacon. Cook as above.

Buttermilk Pancakes (Cont'd.)

Note: To make all varieties from one batter, make Buttermilk Pancakes, without sugar, laddle several servings onto the griddle. Add 1 tbsp. (15 mL) sugar to remaining batter and stir. Laddle several more servings onto the griddle. Add ¼ cup (50 mL) blueberries to remaining batter and stir. Cook several pancakes plain blueberry and several with bacon. Place on a large platter with extra bacon in the center.

Sour Cream-Peach Pancakes

¾ cup	all-purpose flour	175 mL
¼ cup	sugar	50 mL
½ tsp.	baking powder	2 mL
¼-½ tsp.	cinnamon	1-2 mL
1¼ cups	sour cream	300 mL
1	egg, slightly beaten	1
1½ cups	chopped peaches	375 mL
1 tsp.	vanilla	5 mL

In a large bowl, combine dry ingredients. Add sour cream, egg, peaches and vanilla. Stir just until blended. Preheat griddle or frying pan. Grease if necessary. Using ¼ cup (50 mL) of batter at a time, pour onto skillet and flatten slightly. Cook 3-5 minutes. Turn and cook other side.

Yield: 12 medium-size pancakes.

Note: If canned peaches are used, drain thoroughly.

Yogurt Molasses Fruit Crunch

As you eat this nutritious breakfast or snack, think of the various textures and flavors. Think of the healthy ingredients having a positive influence on your body. Smile and have a great day!

½ cup	plain OR fruited yogurt	125 mL
1 tbsp.	molasses	15 mL
2 tbsp.	crunchy cereal (such as granola)	30 mL
2-3	slices fresh OR canned peaches OR fruit of choice	2-3

Place yogurt in a cereal bowl. Add molasses and cereal and stir. Top with peaches.

Serves: 1.

Yogurt Bran Smoothie

Delicious and efficient!

½ cup	plain yogurt	125 mL
2 tbsp.	raw bran	30 mL
2-3 tbsp.	crushed pineapple	30-45 mL

Place yogurt, bran and pineapple in a bowl; stir and enjoy!

Serves: 1.

Eggs, Meat, Poultry & Fish

Omelet Brunch

Great for lunch, brunch or entertaining. Add chilis for a Mexican flavor.

3	eggs	3
1 cup	yogurt OR sour cream	250 mL
¼ cup	finely chopped onion	50 mL
¼ cup	finely chopped green pepper	50 mL
8 oz.	Cheddar cheese, shredded	250 g
8 oz.	Monterey Jack cheese, shredded	250 g
2 x 4 oz.	cans green chilis, seeds removed (optional)	2 x 113 g
2 oz.	jar pimiento (optional)	60 mL

In a large mixing bowl, beat eggs until frothy; beat in yogurt. Add onion and green pepper; blend well. Place 1 layer of green chilis, if using, on the bottom of a well buttered 8 x 8" (20 x 20 cm) pan. Mix cheeses and place half of the mixture over the chilis. Add another layer of chilis, and/or pimiento, then the rest of the cheese. Pour egg mixture evenly over the cheese. Bake, uncovered, at 350°F (180°C) for 45 minutes or until set. Cut into squares and serve hot. Cut into smaller squares to serve as an appetizer.

Yield: 9 slices OR approximately 20 appetizers.

For a different taste, try adding a pinch of cumin and pepper to your scrambled eggs before cooking.

Sour Cream Zucchini Quiche

Real men eat this too!

	unbaked 9" (23 cm) pastry shell	
2 tbsp.	butter	30 mL
4	green onions, finely sliced	4
2	zucchini, cut in thin strips 1" (2.5 cm) long, approximately 2 cups (500 mL)	2
3	eggs	3
¾ cup	sour cream	175 mL
½-1 tsp.	dry mustard	2-5 mL
pinch	each nutmeg, basil, salt and pepper	pinch
1 cup	shredded Gruyère cheese	250 mL

Preheat oven to 400°F (200°C). Lightly prick the pie shell on the bottom and sides with a fork. Bake in the oven for 7 minutes or until lightly browned. Remove and cool at room temperature. Reduce oven heat to 350°F (180°C). Melt butter in a large frying pan, add onion and cook over medium heat for about 5 minutes or until lightly browned. Add the zucchini strips and cook, stirring constantly, for 3-4 minutes. Drain the zucchini and onion well by patting dry with paper towels. In a large bowl, lightly beat the eggs with the sour cream, mustard and seasonings until well mixed. Stir in the cheese, well-drained onion and zucchini. Pour into the prepared pie shell. Bake for 35-45 minutes or until a knife inserted in the center comes out clean. Let stand for 5 minutes before serving.

Serves: 4-6.

Lasagne

A lighter, cheesy lasagne with a pleasant aroma!

12-14	lasagne noodles	12-14
1 tsp.	olive oil	5 mL
1 lb.	lean ground beef OR venison	500 g
½ cup	finely chopped onion	125 mL
14 oz.	can tomatoes, coarsely chopped	398 mL
1 cup	spaghetti sauce	250 mL
1 cup	canned mushroom pieces, drained	250 mL
1-2	garlic cloves, minced	1-2
1 tsp.	each dried basil and oregano	5 mL
1 tsp.	salt OR to taste	5 mL
¼ tsp.	pepper	1 mL
1½ cups	plain yogurt	375 mL
2 cups	cottage cheese	500 mL
1 cup	frozen spinach, drained (optional)	250 mL
1	egg	1
2 cups	shredded mozzarella cheese	500 mL

Cook noodles according to package directions. Add olive oil to water to keep noodles from sticking. Preheat oven to 350°F (180°C). Brown beef and onions in a skillet. Pour off excess fat. Add tomatoes, spaghetti sauce and mushrooms. Stir in garlic, basil, salt, oregano, pepper and yogurt. Heat thoroughly, but do not boil. In a bowl, combine cottage cheese, drained spinach and egg. In a 13 x 9" (33 x 23 cm) baking dish, or 2 smaller pans, alternate layers starting with beef mixture, then noodles, cottage cheese mixture, beef mixture and mozzarella cheese. Repeat layers ending with a cheese layer. Bake in oven for 30 minutes. Remove from oven and let stand 5-10 minutes before serving. Serve with a fresh green salad and warm garlic bread.

Serves: 12-14.

Note: For a less moist Lasagne decrease canned tomato liquid by ¼-½ cup.

Fettuccine Stroganoff

Everyone will come happily to the table when they smell the aroma of this quick and easy stroganoff.

1	pkg. dry onion soup (with Madeira wine)	1
10 oz.	can sliced mushrooms, drained	284 mL
1/8 tsp.	celery salt	0.5 mL
2 tbsp.	Worcestershire sauce	30 mL
¾ cup	water OR red wine	175 mL
3 cups	thinly sliced strips of leftover cooked roast beef	750 mL
1 cup	plain yogurt	250 mL
	regular OR spinach fettuccine (enough for 4 servings)	

Mix together the dry soup mix, canned mushrooms, celery salt, Worcestershire sauce and water or wine. Simmer until bubbly. Add the beef and simmer for 10-15 minutes to blend the flavors. Just before serving, stir in the yogurt. Warm thoroughly. DO NOT BOIL. Cook fettuccine according to package directions. Serve the beef mixture over the fettuccine.

Serves: 4.

Taste your food before salting it. Spices and herbs are healthy salt substitutes. Fresh lemon juice, garlic, onions and basil are natural flavor enhancers.

Roast Beef Stroganoff

Quick and easy for those busy days.

10 oz.	can cream of mushroom soup	284 mL
1 cup	sliced fresh mushrooms OR 1 can mushroom slices, drained	250 mL
2 cups	strips of cooked roast beef	500 mL
1 tsp.	Worcestershire sauce	5 mL
2 tbsp.	ketchup	30 mL
1/8 tsp.	chili powder	0.5 mL
¼ tsp.	garlic powder	1 mL
¾ cup	sour cream	175 mL

Combine all ingredients, except the sour cream. Heat through. Stir in the sour cream and heat for 3 minutes. Do not boil. Serve over hot noodles.

Variation: For a change, serve over cooked spinach.

Serves: 4.

To prevent sticking and to reduce boil overs, add several teaspoons of butter, margarine or vegetable oil to the water before cooking pasta.

Hunter's Ragout

A hearty meal in a pot.

3 tbsp.	olive oil	45 mL
3 tbsp.	butter	45 mL
1½ lbs.	venison OR beef round steak, trimmed and cubed in ½" (1.3 cm) pieces	750 g
2	medium onions, quartered	2
1½ tbsp.	dried chives	22 mL
4 tbsp.	coarsely chopped fresh parsley	60 mL
1 cup	sliced fresh mushrooms OR 10 oz. (284 mL) can mushroom pieces, drained	250 mL
2	medium potatoes, peeled and cubed	2
⅓ cup	white wine OR more	75 mL
1 tsp.	paprika	5 mL
½ tsp.	salt (optional)	2 mL
¼ tsp.	freshly ground black pepper	1 mL
pinch	nutmeg	pinch
⅓ cup	sour cream OR more	75 mL

Place the olive oil in a large heavy skillet over high heat. Add the meat in batches and brown on all sides. Melt the butter in a medium skillet over medium heat. Add onion, chives and 2 tbsp. (30 mL) parsley and cook for 4-5 minutes (or microwave in a microdish on HIGH for 2 minutes, stir, microwave an additional 1½ minutes). Add to meat. Add mushrooms and potatoes and stir well. Add wine, paprika, salt, pepper and nutmeg and stir well. Reduce heat to low, cover and simmer for 55-60 minutes, stirring occasionally. Add 1-2 tbsp. (15-30 mL) more wine, if necessary. Remove from heat and stir in sour cream. Adjust seasoning. Transfer to a serving dish. Garnish with remaining parsley and serve immediately.

Serves: 4-6.

Marinated Steak with Mustard Sauce

This spicy steak and creamy mustard combination are unforgettable!

¾ cup	soy sauce	175 mL
2-3 tbsp.	honey	30-45 mL
⅓ cup	olive oil	75 mL
⅓ cup	lime juice	75 mL
1 cup	chopped onion	250 mL
2 tsp.-2 tbsp.	minced garlic (suggest you start small)	10-30 mL
3 tbsp.	olive oil	45 mL
1 tsp.	curry powder	5 mL
1 tsp.	chili powder	5 mL
1 tsp.	black pepper	5 mL
1	flank steak (not scored), beef round steak OR venison steak	
	Sour Cream Mustard Sauce (recipe follows)	

In a marinating pan (not aluminum), or plastic marinating container, place the soy sauce, honey, ⅓ cup (75 mL) olive oil and lime juice. Stir well to blend. Sauté the onions and garlic in the 3 tbsp. (45 mL) olive oil until the onions are tender. Pour into the marinating container. Add the curry, chili powder and black pepper. Stir well to blend. Place the steak in the marinade. Marinate ~~at room temperature~~ in refrigerator for 24 hours. Turn the steak every few hours. Combine Sour Cream Mustard Sauce ingredients and mix thoroughly. Refrigerate overnight to blend flavors.. Barbecue the steak approximately 6 minutes per side (more or less to your taste). Cut the steak on the diagonal to form thin strips. Serve hot with Mustard Sauce or serve cold on fresh buns with a dab of the sauce or make into the following appetizers.

Serves: 4-5.

Marinated Steak with Mustard Sauce (Cont'd.)

Appetizers

Cut marinated steak warm or cold. If strips are too wide, cut in half. Wrap strips around water chestnuts. Secure with a toothpick. Warm in microwave oven before serving. Place on a serving plate. Serve with a bowl of Mustard Sauce.

Yields: 24-36 appetizers.

See photograph on page 80A.

Sour Cream Mustard Sauce

Excellent as a sauce with venison, beef or ham. Delicious as a dip for cocktail sausages, Marinated Steak page 78 or Sesame Chicken Strips, page 83.

1 cup	sour cream	250 mL
2 tbsp.	Dijon mustard	30 mL
1 tbsp.	soy sauce	15 mL
1 tbsp.	Worcestershire sauce	15 mL
1 tbsp.	chopped onion	15 mL
1-2	garlic cloves, minced	1-2
dash	pepper	dash

In a small bowl, combine all the ingredients and mix well. Refrigerate overnight to blend flavors.

Yield: 1 cup (250 mL).

See photograph on page 80A.

Sour Cream Pork Medallions

The lean pork and creamy sauce are a winning combination.

4	loin boneless rib end chops, 1" (2.5 cm) thick	4
½ cup	water	125 mL
2 tbsp.	ketchup	30 mL
2 tbsp.	brown sugar	30 mL
¼ cup	chopped onion	50 mL
1 tsp.	garlic powder	5 mL
1 tbsp.	flour	15 mL
¼ cup	water	50 mL
½ cup	sour cream	125 mL
	fresh parsley sprigs for garnish (optional)	

In a large skillet, brown pork chops. Add ½ cup (125 mL) water, ketchup, brown sugar, onion and garlic. Cover; simmer for 30-40 minutes or until tender (add a little more water if required). Remove chops to serving platter; keep warm. In a small bowl, combine the flour and ¼ cup (50 mL) water; slowly add to cooking liquid, stirring constantly. Cook until thickened. Stir in sour cream; heat thoroughly. Slice pork into medallions. Serve sauce over medallions. Garnish with parsley.

Serves: 4-6.

Yogurt, buttermilk and sour cream will separate if boiled. The flavor is not affected but the separation can be prevented by adding 1 tsp. (5 mL) flour or cornstarch per cup (250 mL) of sour cream or yogurt.

Sour Cream Mustard Sauce, page 79
Spinach Salad With Buttermilk Dressing, page 36
Oven-Fried Chicken, page 86
Marinated Steak, page 78
Sesame Chicken Strips, page 83
Asparagus Spears With Tomato Sauce, page 40

Ham and Potato Casserole

A quick and tasty luncheon dish.

5	green onions, chopped	5
2	ribs celery, chopped	2
1	garlic clove, minced	1
1 tbsp.	butter	15 mL
3	large potatoes, peeled and cut in ½" (1.3 cm) cubes	3
2 cups	chopped cooked ham	500 mL
10 oz.	can cream of mushroom soup	284 mL
¼ cup	sour cream OR yogurt	50 mL
1 tsp.	thyme	5 mL
dash	ginger	dash
¾-1 cup	grated Cheddar cheese	175-250 mL

Preheat oven to 350°F (180°C). Sauté the green onions, celery and garlic in the butter in a skillet until soft. Put the potatoes into a lightly greased 2-quart (2 L) casserole. Add ham, soup, sour cream, thyme and ginger and stir until well blended. Stir in onion and celery. Cover and bake for approximately 1 hour. Sprinkle cheese on top and bake, uncovered, for 10 minutes.

Serves: 4-6.

For an interesting change, try Curry Sauce on hamburgers. Combine ¼ cup (50 mL) sour cream or yogurt, ¼ cup (50 mL) mayonnaise, ¼ tsp. (1 mL) curry powder and a dash of pepper. Mix well and enjoy a Curry Burger.

Chicken Fingers with Yogurt Sauce

Excellent for unexpected company, because it is so fast and easy to make.

1 tbsp.	butter OR margarine	15 mL
1½ lbs.	chicken breasts, skinned, boned, cut in strips	750 g
¼-½ cup	fruity white wine	50-125 mL
1/8 tsp.	garlic powder	0.5 mL
1 cup	plain yogurt	250 mL
½	green pepper, diced	½
	white and/or wild rice for 4	
1 cup	fresh OR canned mushrooms, sautéed (optional)	
1	peach OR mandarin orange for garnish	1

Melt butter in a frying pan. Add the chicken, brown on all sides on medium heat. Cook until the meat is no longer pink, but do not overcook. Remove the chicken from the pan and set aside. Add the wine to the pan, stir, reduce the heat. Stir in the garlic and yogurt. Place the chicken back in the pan and heat thoroughly, but DO NOT BOIL. Add the green pepper several minutes before serving so that the pepper stays bright and crisp. Serve on a bed of white and/or wild rice (to which fresh or canned sautéed mushrooms have been added). Garnish with peach or orange slices. Accompany this tasty, nutritious dish with a crisp salad.

Serves: 4.

Sesame Chicken Strips

These tender strips can be served as a main course or as a tasty appetizer.

3	whole chicken breasts, skinned, halved and boned	3
1 cup	buttermilk	250 mL
2 tbsp.	lemon juice	30 mL
1 tsp.	celery salt	5 mL
2 tsp.	Worcestershire sauce	10 mL
¼ tsp.	salt	1 mL
¼ tsp.	pepper	1 mL
2-3	garlic cloves, minced	2-3
1 cup	dry bread crumbs (more if necessary)	250 mL
⅓ cup	sesame seeds	75 mL
¼ cup	melted butter OR margarine	50 mL

Cut chicken crosswise in ½" (1.3 cm) wide strips (or use fresh chicken fillets). In a large bowl, combine the buttermilk, lemon juice, celery salt, Worcestershire sauce, salt, pepper and garlic; mix well. Add chicken strips to buttermilk mixture; coat chicken well. Cover; refrigerate overnight. Preheat oven to 350°F (180°C). In a medium bowl, combine the bread crumbs and sesame seeds. Remove chicken from buttermilk mixture; roll in crumb mixture, coating evenly. Lightly grease a 10 x 15" (25 x 38 cm) jelly-roll pan. Arrange chicken in single layer on prepared pan. Spoon butter evenly over the chicken. Bake for 40-45 minutes or until chicken is tender and golden brown. During baking, turn chicken to brown evenly. Serve with Sour Cream Mustard Sauce, page 79, if desired.

Serves: 4-6, or makes 40-50 appetizers.

See photograph on page 80A.

Chicken Breasts with Broccoli

¼ cup	butter	50 mL
¼ cup	finely chopped onion	50 mL
1	garlic clove, minced	1
1½ tsp.	paprika	7 mL
2	whole chicken breasts, halved	2
1	bunch fresh broccoli, cooked crisp	1
2	fresh peaches, halved OR 4 canned peach halves	2
1 cup	yogurt	250 mL
¼ cup	mayonnaise	50 mL
¼ cup	grated Parmesan cheese	50 mL
	salt and pepper to taste	

In a frying pan, melt the butter; add the onions and garlic and sauté for a few minutes. Stir in the paprika. Turn the chicken breasts in the mixture to coat evenly. Place the chicken in a well-greased baking dish. Bake at 375°F (190°C) for 20-30 minutes or until cooked through. Arrange the broccoli in the pan beside the chicken. Place the peaches over the chicken. Mix the yogurt and mayonnaise and spoon over the entire dish. Sprinkle the cheese on top. Put on a low rack and broil for 6-8 minutes. Watch carefully.

Serves: 4.

After taking antibiotics, eat yogurt to help restore beneficial intestinal bacteria.

Pasta Chicken

A convenience dish that is simple and flavorful.

5 tbsp.	flour	75 mL
1 tsp.	paprika	5 mL
¼ tsp.	pepper	1 mL
3	large whole chicken breasts, washed and dried	3
¼ cup	sunflower oil	50 mL
½ lb.	fresh mushrooms, sliced OR 10 oz. (284 mL) can sliced mushrooms, drained	250 g
10 oz.	can cream of chicken soup	284 mL
2 cups	chicken OR vegetable stock	500 mL
1/8 tsp.	rubbed rosemary	0.5 mL
1 tsp.	marjoram	5 mL
2 cups	sour cream	500 mL
3 cups	cooked macaroni OR noodles	750 mL
2 cups	frozen mixed peas and carrots	500 mL

Mix flour, paprika and pepper. Coat chicken pieces on both sides. Brown on all sides in hot oil in frying pan. Remove from pan and keep warm. Sauté the mushrooms in the same pan in which the chicken was cooked. Pour off excess oil, if necessary. Stir in undiluted soup, stock, rosemary and marjoram until mixture is smooth. Add sour cream; heat but DO NOT BOIL. Arrange macaroni or noodles in a greased 13 x 9 x 2" (38 x 23 x 5 cm) baking dish. Add peas and carrots and half of the sour cream mixture and stir. Arrange chicken breasts on top. Cover with remaining sour cream mixture. Cover with foil and bake at 350°F (180°C) for 1 hour. Remove the cover and bake an additional 15-20 minutes until chicken is tender. Freezes well.

Serves: 6.

Oven-Fried Chicken

The crisp coating and tender, moist chicken produce a mouth-watering delight.

¼ cup	all-purpose flour	50 mL
¼ tsp.	thyme	1 mL
½ tsp.	ground sage	2 mL
1/8 tsp.	garlic powder	0.5 mL
½ tsp.	salt (optional)	2 mL
¼ tsp.	pepper	1 mL
1	small chicken, cut in 8 pieces and skinned, if preferred	1
½ cup	buttermilk OR yogurt	125 mL
1 cup	crushed corn flakes (more if necessary)	250 mL
¼ cup	butter, melted (optional)	50 mL

Combine flour, thyme, sage, garlic, salt and pepper in a shallow bowl. Wash chicken and pat dry. Turn chicken pieces in mixture until well coated. Pour buttermilk into a second bowl. Dip the chicken in the buttermilk and then roll in the corn flakes. Place on a rack in a shallow pan. Drizzle with the butter (optional). Bake 1 hour at 375-400°F (190-200°C), turning occasionally or until the chicken is tender when tested with a fork and the coating is crisp.

Serves: 6.

Variation: As an appetizer, use mini drumsticks. Drizzle with honey after baking.

See photograph on page 80A.

Chicken Paprika

Hungarian in origin, this chicken dish is tender and creamy!

4	whole chicken legs, halved (thighs and drumsticks	4
3 tbsp.	olive oil	45 mL
1	large onion, finely chopped	1
1/8 tsp.	salt (optional)	0.5 mL
1 tbsp.	paprika	15 mL
¾ cup	water, divided	175 mL
1½ cups	sour cream	375 mL
1 tbsp.	flour	15 mL
1	each green and red pepper, sliced in rings, for garnish (optional)	1

Wash chicken and pat dry with a paper towel. In a large frying pan, heat the olive oil over medium heat for approximately 1 minute. Add the onions and sauté until transparent. Place the chicken in the pan and cook, turning until browned on all sides. Sprinkle the salt and paprika over the chicken. Add ½ cup (125 mL) of the water. Cover and bring to a boil. Reduce heat and simmer for about 30 minutes. Add an additional small amount of water, if necessary. In a small bowl, combine the sour cream, flour and remaining ¼ cup (50 mL) of water. Pour this mixture over the chicken and stir. Simmer, uncovered, for an additional 5 minutes. Place chicken on a serving dish. Pour the sauce over the chicken and garnish with the pepper rings or strips.

Serves: 4.

Tandoori-Style BBQ Chicken Legs

Yogurt adds a wonderful flavor to this East Indian dish, as well as tenderizing the meat.

4-6	whole chicken legs OR breasts, skinned	4-6
3 tbsp.	lime juice	45 mL
1 tsp.	salt	5 mL
1 cup	plain yogurt	250 mL
¼ tsp.	coriander	1 mL
¼ tsp.	cumin	1 mL
¼ tsp.	nutmeg	1 mL
¼ tsp.	cinnamon	1 mL
¼ tsp.	black pepper	1 mL
1	garlic clove, minced (optional)	1
	fresh lemon and lime twists and parsley sprigs for garnish	

To skin the chicken legs, hold the chicken thigh in one hand and pull the skin back toward and over the leg. Cut several diagonal slits in each of the chicken pieces. Rub the chicken pieces with lime juice and salt and place in a marinating container. Combine the yogurt and spices; pour over the chicken and cover. Refrigerate for 24 hours. Turn the chicken several times. Preheat the barbecue and place the chicken on the grill. Turn as required and baste with the marinade. Continue barbecuing until the juice runs clear, when a fork is inserted into the thickest part of the chicken flesh. This dish may also be baked in a 350-375°F (180-190°C) oven, 40-50 minutes, or until tender. Garnish with lemon and lime twists and parsley sprigs.

Serves: 4-6.

Fish Fillets in Creamy Sauce

1	large onion, sliced	1
2	tomatoes, thickly sliced	2
2 lbs.	fish fillets	1 kg
	lemon juice	
	pepper and paprika to taste	
½ cup	grated Parmesan cheese	125 mL
1 cup	sour cream OR yogurt	250 mL
1 tsp.	flour (optional)	5 mL
1 tbsp.	butter	15 mL
	parsley sprigs and lemon twists for garnish	

In a greased baking dish, arrange onion and tomatoes. Place fish on top. Sprinkle with lemon juice, pepper and paprika. Combine cheese, sour cream and flour. Pour over fish. Dot with butter. Bake in a 400°F (200°C) oven until fish flakes easily with a fork, about 15 minutes. Garnish with parsley and lemon twists.

Serves: 4-6.

Fish is cooked when it loses its translucence and flakes easily with a fork.

Cheesy Noodles

This pasta dish is nutritious and simple to make.

8 oz.	medium egg noodles (approx. 3½ cups)	250 g
2	garlic cloves, minced	2
¼ cup	chopped onion	50 mL
1 cup	fresh mushrooms, sliced	250 mL
2 tbsp.	butter	30 mL
1½ cups	sour cream	375 mL
1½ cups	cottage cheese	375 mL
½-1 cup	shredded Cheddar cheese	125-250 mL
1 cup	tuna, salmon OR cubed ham (optional)	250 mL
	salt and pepper to taste	
	buttered bread crumbs	
	Parmesan cheese, grated	

Cook the noodles according to package directions and drain. Sauté the garlic, onions and mushrooms in the butter. In a 3-quart (3 L) casserole, thoroughly combine the noodles, mushroom mixture, sour cream, cottage cheese, Cheddar cheese, tuna, salt and pepper. Top with buttered bread crumbs and bake at 350°F (180°C) for approximately 30 minutes, or until thoroughly warmed. Sprinkle the top with Parmesan cheese before serving.

Serves: 6-10.

Serve sour cream on hot egg noodles seasoned with salt, pepper and poppy seeds.

Desserts

Georgian Bay Apple Pie

This pie is as tasty as the area is beautiful!

	unbaked 9" (23 cm) pie shell	
1 cup	sugar	250 mL
2 tbsp.	flour	30 mL
½ tsp.	cinnamon	2 mL
¼ tsp.	nutmeg	1 mL
¾ cup	sour cream	175 mL
5-6 cups	peeled sliced apples	1.25-1.5 L

Topping

½ cup	brown sugar	125 mL
½ cup	flour	125 mL
1 tsp.	cinnamon	5 mL
⅓ cup	butter	75 mL

Prepare pie shell using your favorite recipe or try Sour Cream Pastry, page 94. Combine sugar, flour and cinnamon. Blend in the nutmeg and sour cream. Add the apples and combine to coat well. Put mixture into the pie shell and prepare topping. Combine the brown sugar, flour and cinnamon. Cut in the butter to make a crumbly mixture. Sprinkle over the apple mixture. Bake at 400°F (200°C) for 10 minutes; lower heat to 350°F (180°C) and bake for an additional 30 minutes.

Serves: 6.

Variation: Use ¼ cup (50 mL) flour, plus ¼ cup (50 mL) rolled oats in the topping.

An apple a day still helps to keep the Doctor away. Fresh fruits and vegetables are important to our daily diets.

Rhubarb and Strawberry Pie

Always a favorite combination.

	unbaked 10" (25 cm) pie shell	
4 cups	diced rhubarb	1 L
1-2 cups	sliced strawberries	250-500 mL
⅓ cup	flour	75 mL
1½ cups	white sugar	375 mL
1 cup	sour cream	250 mL

Topping

½ cup	all-purpose flour	125 mL
½ cup	brown sugar	125 mL
¼ cup	soft butter	50 mL

Prepare pastry. Arrange fruit in the pie shell. Mix the ⅓ cup (75 mL) flour and sugar and blend in the sour cream. Pour evenly over the fruit. Blend the topping ingredients together until crumbly and then sprinkle over the pie. Bake at 450°F (230°C) for 15 minutes. Reduce oven to 350°F (180°C) and bake for an additional 30 minutes.

Serves: 6.

Try brushing the bottom crust of a fruit pie with egg whites before filling, to help prevent sogginess.

Raspberry Pie

Who can resist a scrumptious raspberry pie?

	unbaked 10" (25 cm) pie shell	
2½ cups	fresh OR frozen raspberries	625 mL
½ cup	all-purpose flour	125 mL
1 cup	sugar, reserve 2 tbsp. (30 mL) for top	250 mL
1½ cups	yogurt	375 mL
1½ cups	sour cream	375 mL
2 tsp.	vanilla extract	10 mL
1 cup	white bread crumbs	250 mL
3 tbsp.	melted butter	45 mL
	whipped cream for garnish	

Prepare pastry. Spread raspberries over bottom of pie shell. Stir together the flour and 7/8 cup (200 mL) sugar then add the yogurt sour cream and vanilla. Pour over berries. Mix together the bread crumbs and melted butter. Sprinkle crumb mixture over pie. Sprinkle the reserved sugar on top. Bake at 400°F (200°C) for 15 minutes. Reduce oven heat to 375°F (190°C) and continue baking for 35 minutes or until brown on top. Cool and serve as is or with whipped cream.

Serves: 6.

Sour Cream Pastry

This pastry goes especially well with apple pie filling.

2½ cups	all-purpose flour	625 mL
½ tsp.	salt	2 mL
1 cup	shortening OR lard	250 mL
6 tbsp. +	sour cream OR yogurt	90 mL +
	sugar and flour	

Sour Cream Pastry (Cont'd.)

Sift flour and salt. Blend in shortening with a pastry blender until particles are very small. Mix in sour cream. Mixture will form into a smooth ball. Divide dough in half. Roll dough on tea towel or pastry cloth sprinkled generously with flour and sugar. Roll to required size.

For baked pie shell, prick dough and bake at 425°F (220°C) for 10-15 minutes. Cool pastry before adding filling.

Yield: 2 single-crust shells OR 1 double-crust pie shell.

Sour Cream Blueberry Pie

Fast and simple. Try using various fruits such as kiwi, mandarin oranges and raspberries to create new and interesting variations.

1½ cups	graham wafer crumbs	375 mL
½ cup	brown sugar	125 mL
6 tbsp.	melted butter	90 mL
2 cups	blueberries (reserve several for garnish)	500 mL
8 oz.	jar red currant jelly	250 mL
½-1 cup	sour cream	125-250 mL

Mix wafer crumbs, sugar and butter. Press into an 9" or 10" (23-25 cm) pie plate. Bake at 375°F (190°C) for 15 minutes. Fill crust with blueberries. Heat the jelly and pour evenly over the berries. Cover with sour cream. Chill for several hours. Keep refrigerated until you are ready to serve. Place reserved berries decoratively on top of the sour cream.

Serves: 6.

Peaches and Cream Pie

An unbeatable team — peaches and cream.

	unbaked 9" (23 cm) pie shell	
3 cups	peeled, sliced peaches	750 mL
½ cup	white sugar	125 mL
½ tsp.	cinnamon	2 mL
3 tbsp.	flour	45 mL
pinch	salt	pinch
1 cup	yogurt OR sour cream	250 mL
¼ cup	brown sugar	50 mL

Prepare pastry. Arrange peaches in the pastry shell. Combine white sugar, flour, cinnamon and yogurt or sour cream (or use half yogurt and half sour cream). Beat until smooth then spoon over peaches. Bake at 425°F (220°C) for 15 minutes. Reduce heat to 325°F (160°C) and continue baking for approximately 30 minutes, until crust is browned and the filling has set. Sprinkle brown sugar over the top. Return to the oven to melt the sugar slightly. Excellent served warm or cold.

Serves: 6.

For a zippy dessert add a tablespoon (15 mL) of liqueur to a dish of plain yogurt. Top with fruit or nuts.

Pineapple Sour Cream Pie

	baked 9" (23 cm) pie shell	
¾ cup	white sugar	175 mL
¼ cup	all-purpose flour	50 mL
2½ cups	crushed pineapple, undrained	625 mL
1 cup	sour cream	250 mL
1 tbsp.	lemon juice	15 mL
2	egg yolks, slightly beaten	2
2	egg whites	2
½ tsp.	vanilla	2 mL
¼ tsp.	cream of tartar	1 mL
¼ cup	sugar	50 mL

Prepare pastry. In a saucepan, combine sugar and flour. Stir in pineapple, sour cream and lemon juice. Cook until mixture thickens and comes to a boil. Cook 2 additional minutes. Stir small amount of hot mixture into egg yolks and return to filling. Cook 2 minutes longer. Cool to room temperature and spoon into baked pie shell. Beat egg whites with vanilla and cream of tartar until soft peaks form. Gradually add ¼ cup (50 mL) of sugar, beating until stiff peaks form. Spread meringue over pie, making sure all edges are sealed with meringue. Bake meringue at 350°F (180°C) for 10-12 minutes. Cool to room temperature then refrigerate several hours or overnight and serve chilled.

Serves: 6.

Use a buttered knife to slice through soft pies and meringue.

Lemon Yogurt Meringue Pie

Absolutely delicious! The yogurt smooths the tart lemon taste. The filling may also be served as a pudding.

	baked 9" OR 10" (23-25 cm) pie shell	
4-5 tbsp.	cornstarch OR flour	60-75 mL
1 cup	sugar	250 mL
1¼ cups	hot water	300 mL
2	egg yolks, slightly beaten	2
2 tsp.	butter	10 mL
¼ cup	lemon juice	50 mL
1-2 tsp.	grated lemon rind	5-10 mL
1 cup	plain yogurt	250 mL
3	egg whites	3
6 tbsp.	sugar	90 mL
¼-½ tsp.	lemon juice OR vinegar	1-2 mL

Prepare pastry. In a saucepan, mix the cornstarch and 1 cup (250 mL) sugar; add the hot water and stir to dissolve the sugar. Cook over medium heat until thick and transparent. Stir gently, as required, to prevent sticking. After the mixture is clear, simmer for about 5 minutes. Cool slightly. Add a little of the hot mixture to the beaten yolks. Stir the warmed egg mixture quickly into the starch mixture. Continue to cook for a few minutes over low heat. Remove from heat, add the butter, lemon juice and lemon rind. Stir gently until blended and butter has melted. Cool, then fold in the yogurt. Pour into the pie shell. Prepare meringue by beating the egg whites until stiff. Gradually add the 6 tbsp. (90 mL) sugar; beat well. Add lemon juice and beat again. Cover pie with meringue, spreading it to reach all edges of the pie crust. Preheat oven to 350°F (180°C). Bake pie for approximately 5-10 minutes or until the meringue is golden brown. Allow meringue to cool at room temperature, in a draft-free place, then chill the pie several hours in the refrigerator before serving.

Serves: 6.

Maple Cream Pie

Maple syrup is truly a Canadian treat. This is a "sweet tooth" satisfier.

	unbaked 8" (20 cm) pie shell	
2 tbsp.	soft butter	30 mL
2	egg yolks	2
1 cup	maple syrup	250 mL
½ cup	sour cream	125 mL
¼ cup	flour	50 mL
1 tsp.	vinegar	5 mL
1 tsp.	vanilla	5 mL
2	egg whites	2
¼ tsp.	salt	1 mL
4 tbsp.	sugar	60 mL
	shaved maple sugar for garnish	

Prepare pastry. Beat together the butter, egg yolks, syrup, sour cream, flour, vinegar and vanilla. Pour into the pie shell. Bake at 425°F (220°C) for 20 minutes. Reduce heat to 325°F (160°C) and continue to bake for another 30 minutes or until a toothpick inserted in the center comes out clean. Beat egg whites with salt and sugar until stiff. Spoon over pie, making sure all edges are sealed. Bake at 350°F (180°C) for 15 minutes until browned lightly. Serve at room temperature. Sprinkle with shaved maple sugar.

Serves: 6.

Drink 6-8 glasses of water daily, the body likes it!

Welsh Pie (Sour Cream Raisin Pie)

	baked 9" (23 cm) pie shell	
1 cup	chopped raisins	250 mL
1 cup	sugar	250 mL
1 cup	sour cream	250 mL
4	eggs, separated	4
½ tsp.	cloves	2 mL
4 tbsp.	sugar	60 mL
	chopped nuts for garnish	

Prepare pie shell. Boil raisins for 10 minutes in just enough water to cover. Mix the 1 cup (250 mL) sugar, sour cream, egg yolks and cloves, then add to boiled raisins (most of liquid will disappear). Cook slowly for 5 minutes or until thickened. Pour into baked pie shell. Beat egg whites until stiff and then beat in 4 tbsp. (60 mL) sugar. Cover the pie with the meringue* and sprinkle with the nuts. Brown meringue in a 350°F (180°C) oven for approximately 5 minutes or until peaks are golden brown. Refrigerate until serving time.

Serves: 6.

*Meringue will shrink and pull away from pie crust during baking if all pie crust edges are not completely sealed with meringue. Cool meringue-topped pies at room temperature in a draft-free place, to avoid shrinkage.

Pumpkin Pie

A Mennonite-style pumpkin pie. Don't just save this for Hallowe'en. Enjoy pumpkin all year 'round.

	unbaked 9" OR 10" (23-25 cm) pie shell	
2 cups	mashed pumpkin	500 mL
1 cup	sugar	250 mL
1 cup	sour cream	250 mL
3	eggs, well-beaten	3
2 tbsp.	molasses	30 mL
2 tbsp.	melted butter	30 mL
1 tsp.	vanilla	5 mL
½ tsp.	each nutmeg and cinnamon	2 mL
1/8 tsp.	cloves	0.5 mL
	whipped cream	
1 tbsp.	chopped preserved ginger for garnish	15 mL

Prepare pastry. Thoroughly combine pumpkin, sugar, sour cream, eggs, molasses, butter, vanilla, nutmeg, cinnamon and cloves and pour into the unbaked pie shell. Bake at 350°F (180°C) for 45 minutes or until well set. Garnish with whipped cream and ginger.

Serves: 6.

Pumpkin is a good source of Vitamin A.

Sour Cream Tarts

All your friends will ask for this recipe!

16	large unbaked tart shells OR 3-4 dozen mini tart shells	16
1	egg, well beaten	1
1 cup	white sugar	250 mL
1 cup	sour cream	250 mL
1 cup	raisins	250 mL
pinch	salt (optional)	pinch
½ tsp.	vanilla	2 mL

Prepare pastry. Blend the egg and sugar. Then fold in the sour cream, raisins, salt and vanilla. Spoon into unbaked tart shells and fill ⅔ full. Bake at 375°F (190°C) for approximately 20 minutes. Watch carefully.

Yield: 16 large OR 36-48 mini tarts.

Try using cold coffee (for a mocha flavor) instead of water, when making a chocolate cake mix.

Use cocoa to dust the baking pan when baking a chocolate or mocha cake.

Luscious Chocolate Cake

This is a delicious, moist cake.

½ cup	butter OR margarine	125 mL
1½ cups	white sugar	375 mL
1 tsp.	vanilla	5 mL
2	eggs	2
2	squares unsweetened chocolate, melted	2
2 cups	sifted flour	500 mL
1½ tsp.	baking soda	7 mL
½ tsp.	salt (optional)	2 mL
1½ cups	buttermilk, sour cream OR yogurt	375 mL

Cream butter, sugar and vanilla. Mix in eggs and add chocolate. Sift dry ingredients and add alternately with buttermilk (or sour cream or yogurt) to the chocolate mixture. Bake in a greased and floured 9 x 13" (23 x 33 cm) pan at 350°F (180°C) for approximately 40 minutes. This cake does not require icing, however, you can try Chocolate Buttermilk Icing, page 104, for a treat and top with ¼-½ cup (50-125 mL) chopped walnuts.

Serves: 12-16.

Chocolate Leaves

For special occasions make chocolate leaves to decorate desserts. Choose waxy leaves with visible veins. Wash and carefully dry the leaves. Melt tempered "coating" chocolate (available at specality stores) and paint the backs of the leaves with chocolate, using a pastry brush. Place on wax paper on a cookie sheet. Repeat painting process several times. Place in refrigerator to harden. To remove the chocolate from the leaves, slide the tip of a sharp knife between the leaf and chocolate near the stem. Gently pull the leaf away from the chocolate. Place over a rounded spoon handle to give the leaf a nice curve. Decorate the cake with these delicate leaves and refrigerate until serving time.

Creamy Chocolate Icing

1 cup	chocolate chips	250 mL
¼ cup	cocoa	50 mL
¾ cup	buttermilk	175 mL
½ cup	butter	125 mL
3 cups	sifted icing sugar	750 mL
1¼ tsp.	vanilla	6 mL

Place chocolate chips, cocoa, buttermilk and butter in a microwave dish. Microwave on MEDIUM until chocolate is just melted (40-60 seconds). Watch closely. Mix thoroughly. Cool slightly. (Alternately, melt in the top of a double boiler.) Beat in icing sugar and vanilla. Chill until spreadable.

Yield: Sufficient to ice top, center and sides of an 8" (20 cm) layer cake — approximately 2½ cups.

Chocolate Buttermilk Icing

6 tbsp.	buttermilk	90 mL
½ cup	butter, softened	125 mL
4 tbsp.	cocoa	60 mL
2-3 cups	sifted icing sugar	500-750 mL
1 cup	chopped walnuts (optional)	250 mL

Bring first 3 ingredients to a boil. Remove from heat. Add icing sugar and nuts. Stir until smooth then use to glaze or ice a cake.

Yield: Approximately 3 cups (750 mL).

Maple Chocolate Chip Cake

This cake is easy to make, flavorful and superb for luncheons or the lunchbox.

½ cup	butter	125 mL
⅔ cup	sugar	150 mL
1 tsp.	vanilla	5 mL
⅔ cup	maple syrup	150 mL
2	eggs	2
1¾ cups	sifted flour	425 mL
1 tsp.	baking soda	5 mL
½ tsp.	baking powder	2 mL
½ tsp.	salt (optional)	2 mL
⅔ cup	buttermilk	150 mL
1 cup	semisweet chocolate chips	250 mL

Cream the butter thoroughly; then add the sugar gradually, until mixture is light. Add the vanilla, maple syrup and eggs, 1 at a time, beating well after each addition. Sift the flour, baking soda, baking powder and salt together. Add the flour alternately with the buttermilk to the butter mixture and blend well. Stir in the chocolate chips. Spoon the batter into a greased and floured bundt pan or an 8 x 8" (20 x 20 cm) cake pan. Bake at 350°F (180°C) for 20 minutes. Reduce oven temperature to 325°F (160°C) and continue baking until a cake tester inserted in the center comes out clean, approximately 45 minutes.

Serves: 10-12.

A cake will frost much easier if it is frozen or almost frozen before applying the icing.

Yogurt Cake

Excellent as a base for trifle too!

3 cups	all-purpose flour	750 mL
3 tsp.	baking powder	15 mL
½ tsp.	baking soda	2 mL
1½ cups	sugar	375 mL
1 cup	melted butter	250 mL
5	eggs	5
1 cup	yogurt	250 mL
1	lemon, grated rind of	1

Sift together the flour, baking powder and baking soda. With an electric mixer, blend the sugar and butter. Beat at medium speed for about 2 minutes. Add the eggs, 1 at a time, then the yogurt, with the mixer at the same speed. Slowly add the flour mixture, until the batter has a smooth consistency. Fold in the lemon rind. Pour the batter into a 9 x 9" (23 x 23 cm) greased and floured cake pan. Bake at 350°F (180°C) for 45 minutes, or until a cake tester inserted in the center comes out clean. Serve as is or ice with Lemon Glaze, below.

Yield: Approximately 24 — 1 x 3" (2.5-7 cm) pieces.

Lemon Glaze

2 cups	icing sugar	500 mL
1 tbsp.	soft butter	15 mL
1 tsp.	lemon juice	5 mL
2-3 tbsp.	hot water	30-45 mL

Combine all ingredients, adding enough water to make a thick glaze.

Yield: Approximately 2 cups (500 mL).

Rhubarb Cake

This cake is self-iced and is delicious served as is, or with ice cream.

½ cup	shortening OR vegetable oil	125 mL
1½ cups	brown sugar	375 mL
1	egg	1
1 tsp.	vanilla	5 mL
2 cups	sifted all-purpose flour	500 mL
1 tsp.	baking powder	5 mL
1 tsp.	baking soda	5 mL
1 cup	sour cream	250 mL
2 cups	diced rhubarb	500 mL
½ cup	chopped nuts	125 mL

Topping

1 tbsp.	butter	15 mL
½ cup	brown sugar	125 mL
2 tsp.	cinnamon	10 mL

Thoroughly cream the shortening while gradually adding the sugar. Add the egg and beat until light then add vanilla. Measure flour, baking powder and baking soda together. Add dry ingredients alternately with the sour cream, in 3 equal parts, to the sugar mixture. Mix just until blended — batter will be fairly thick. Stir in rhubarb and nuts. Spread in a 9 x 13" (23 x 33 cm) pan (or smaller). Spread well into the corners. Mix topping ingredients together and sprinkle over the cake batter. Bake at 350°F (180°C) for 35-45 minutes.

Yield: Approximately 15-20 pieces.

Banana Split Cake

Always a favorite with children. They will think of other toppings.

2 cups	cake & pastry flour OR 2 cups (500 mL) less 4 tbsp. (60 mL) all-purpose flour	500 mL
1 tsp.	baking soda	5 mL
2 tsp.	baking powder	10 mL
⅔ cup	shortening	150 mL
1½ cups	lightly packed brown sugar	375 mL
⅔ cup	buttermilk	150 mL
1 cup	mashed banana	250 mL
2	eggs	2

Topping

sliced bananas
butterscotch OR chocolate sauce
chopped nuts

Preheat oven to 350°F (180°C). Grease a 9 x 9" (23 x 23 cm) cake pan and dust lightly with flour. Sift together into a mixing bowl, the flour, baking soda and baking powder. Add shortening, brown sugar and buttermilk. Beat with an electric mixer for 2 minutes at medium speed. Add mashed banana and eggs. Beat for an additional 2 minutes. Turn into pan. Bake for 45-50 minutes or until a cake tester inserted in the center comes out clean. Cool. Serve as is, with Butter Icing, page 66, or split horizontally and insert a layer of sliced bananas. Top with sliced bananas and drizzle with sauce. Sprinkle with nuts.

Yield: Approximately 9-12 pieces.

Bananas are an excellent source of potassium.

Raspberry Yogurt Flan

A light, quick and colorful dessert for family or entertaining.

1½ cups	chocolate graham wafer crumbs	375 mL
¼ cup	sugar	50 mL
½ cup	butter OR margarine	125 mL
2	envelopes gelatin	2
⅓ cup	hot water	75 mL
3 cups	yogurt	750 mL
2 tbsp.	sugar	30 mL
19 oz.	can raspberry pie filling	540 mL
	whipped cream and fresh raspberries OR	
	chocolate curls for garnish	

Combine the crumbs, ¼ cup (50 mL) sugar and butter. Blend well. Press into the bottom and 1" (2.5 cm) up the sides of a 9" (23 cm) springform pan. Bake at 375°F (190°C) for 8 minutes. Cool. In a saucepan, sprinkle the gelatin over the hot water. Heat to dissolve. Combine the yogurt and 2 tbsp. (30 mL) of sugar. Stir the gelatin and ¾ cup (175 mL) raspberry pie filling into the yogurt. Pour into the crust and chill for about 30 minutes. Spoon the remaining pie filling over the yogurt layer and refrigerate until serving time. Garnish the top with whipped cream and fresh raspberries in season or chocolate curls.

Serves: 10-12.

Keep club soda on hand to bubble out wine, juice or blood stains. Blot dry with a paper towel.

Peach Yogurt Fantasy

Delicious for entertaining or family meals.

Crust

1¼ cups	all-purpose flour	300 mL
1 tsp.	baking powder	5 mL
1 tbsp.	sugar	15 mL
½ cup	butter	125 mL
1	egg, slightly beaten	1
1 tbsp.	milk	15 mL

Filling

4-6	peaches, peeled and sliced OR 1 can peach slices, drained	4-6
1	egg, slightly beaten	1
1 cup	yogurt	250 mL
1½ tbsp.	flour	22 mL
¾ cup	sugar OR ¼-½ cup (50-125 mL) if using canned peaches	175 mL

Topping

½ cup	brown sugar	125 mL
2 tbsp.	softened butter	30 mL
2 tbsp.	flour	30 mL
½ tsp.	cinnamon	2 mL

To make the crust, mix the flour, baking powder and sugar. Cut in the butter as with pie pastry. Mix together the egg and milk and add to the flour mixture. Press into the bottom and sides of a 8 x 12" (20 x 30 cm) pan. Prepare filling by placing the peach slices over the crust. Mix egg, yogurt, flour and sugar and pour over the fruit. Prepare the topping by creaming the sugar and butter. Cut in the flour and cinnamon and then sprinkle over the fruit filling. Bake at 350°F (180°C) for 45 minutes until fruit is baked and topping is a light brown.

Serves: 10-12.

Key Lime Cheesecake

If you like Key Lime Pie, you'll love this creamy, moist cheesecake!

⅓ cup	melted butter OR margarine	75 mL
1¼ cups	graham wafer crumbs	300 mL
¼ cup	sugar	50 mL
8 oz.	pkg. cream cheese	250 g
10½ oz.	can sweetened condensed milk	300 mL
1 cup	sour cream OR yogurt	250 mL
3	eggs	3
¾ cup	concentrated lime juice	175 mL
½ cup	sugar	125 mL
2-3 tsp.	grated lime rind (optional)	30-45 mL

Topping

½ cup	sour cream	125 mL
1-2 tbsp.	fresh lime juice	15-30 mL
1½ tbsp.	sugar	22 mL
	lime slices dipped in sugar for garnish	

Preheat oven to 350°F (180°C). Combine butter, crumbs and ¼ cup (50 mL) sugar then pat firmly into the bottom and 1" (2.5 cm) up the sides of a 9" (23 cm) springform pan. Refrigerate until ready to use. In a large mixing bowl, beat cheese until fluffy. Add condensed milk and sour cream; beat until smooth. Add eggs, lime juice, ½ cup (125 mL) sugar and lime rind; mix well. Pour into prepared pan. Bake 50-55 minutes or until cake springs back when lightly touched. Cool to room temperature. Chill. Remove sides of pan. Combine topping ingredients thoroughly and spread on cooled cheesecake. Garnish with lime slices dipped in sugar. Refrigerate until serving time.

Yield: 14-18 slices.

Chocolate Cheesecake

For the chocolate lovers, this is a triple delight!

Crust

1¼ cups	chocolate wafer crumbs OR 1 cup (250 mL) graham wafer crumbs plus ¼ cup (50 mL) cocoa	300 mL
2 tbsp.	sugar	30 mL
¼ cup	melted butter	50 mL

Filling

1 lb.	cream cheese	500 g
½ cup	sugar	125 mL
2	large eggs	2
6 oz.	semisweet chocolate, melted, cooled	170 g
½ tsp.	almond extract	2 mL
1 tsp.	vanilla	5 mL
⅔ cup	yogurt or sour cream	150 mL

Topping

2 oz.	semisweet chocolate	55 g
1 tsp.	shortening	5 mL
	seasonal fresh fruit	

Combine crumbs, sugar and melted butter. Press into the bottom and halfway up sides of a buttered 8-9" (20-23 cm) springform pan. Chill while making filling. Beat cream cheese well until smooth. Beat in sugar gradually. Beat in eggs, 1 at a time, at low speed. Add cooled chocolate, flavorings and yogurt. Beat at low speed until thoroughly blended. Pour into prepared pan. Bake at 300°F (150°C) for 1 hour, turn off heat and leave cake in oven for an additional hour. Cool in pan at room temperature, then cool at least 24 hours in the refrigerator. For topping, melt chocolate with shortening then spread or drizzle over top of cheesecake. Garnish with fresh fruit, strawberries, raspberries, etc. to enhance and complement the rich chocolate flavors.

Chocolate Cheesecake, page 112

Chocolate Cheesecake (Cont'd.)

Yield: 14-18 rich slices.

Variation: To decorate this cheesecake as photographed, make chocolate leaves as described on page 103.

See photograph on page 112A.

Welsh Cakes

These tempting cookies are easy to make and add a pleasant aroma to the house while cooking.

3 cups	all-purpose flour	750 mL
¾ cup	sugar	175 mL
½ tsp.	baking soda	2 mL
2 tsp.	nutmeg, well rounded	10 mL
1½ tsp.	baking powder	7 mL
1 cup	butter OR margarine	250 mL
1 cup	currants	250 mL
2	eggs, beaten	2
5 tbsp.	buttermilk	75 mL

Sift the dry ingredients into a large bowl. Cut in butter, as with pastry. Stir in the currants. Make a well in the center of the dry ingredients. Add the egg and buttermilk. Combine thoroughly. Refrigerate for 1 hour, then roll out ¼" (1 cm) thick. Cut in 1½" (4 cm) rounds with a floured cookie cutter or juice glass. Bake on a slightly greased, hot griddle until lightly brown. Flip and brown the other side.

Yield: 5-6 dozen.

Buttermilk Chocolate Chip Cookies

The soft texture creates an interesting cookie.

1 cup	shortening	250 mL
2 cups	sugar	500 mL
2	eggs	2
1½ cups	buttermilk	375 mL
2 tsp.	vanilla	10 mL
4 cups	sifted flour	1 L
1 tsp.	baking soda	5 mL
1 tsp.	baking powder	5 mL
½ tsp.	salt (optional)	2 mL
2 cups	chocolate chips	500 mL

Cream shortening, sugar and eggs until light and fluffy. Beat in buttermilk and vanilla. Sift together flour, baking soda, baking powder and salt. Stir into batter. Stir in chocolate chips. Drop by rounded teaspoonfuls (5 mL) onto greased cookie sheets. Bake at 375°F (190°C) for 10-12 minutes. Cookies should brown around the edge but not in the center.

Yield: 6 dozen cookies.

Whole-wheat flour should be refrigerated or frozen for longer storage.

Spicy Drop Cookies

1 cup	softened butter	250 mL
2	eggs	2
1½ cups	brown sugar	375 mL
1 tsp.	vanilla	5 mL
2½ cups	flour	625 mL
1 tsp.	baking soda	5 mL
½ tsp.	ground cloves	2 mL
⅔ cup	buttermilk	150 mL
1 lb.	dates, chopped	500 g
½ cup	chopped walnuts	125 mL

Cream together the butter, eggs, sugar and vanilla. Sift the dry ingredients and add alternately to the creamed mixture with the buttermilk. Stir in the dates and nuts. Drop by spoonfuls onto an ungreased cookie sheet. Bake at 350°F (180°C) for approximately 12-15 minutes. Cookies are done when brown around the edges.

Yield: 4 dozen.

One cup (250 mL) whole-wheat flour can be substituted for 1 cup (250 mL) all-purpose flour.

One cup (250 mL) all-purpose flour can be substituted for 1 cup (250 mL) plus 2 tbsp. (30 mL) cake and pastry flour; 1 cup (250 mL) minus 2 tbsp. (30 mL) all-purpose flour = 1 cup (250 mL) cake and pastry flour).

Buttermilk Pralines

A southern treat that's sinfully delicious!

2 cups	granulated sugar	500 mL
1 tsp.	baking soda	5 mL
1 cup	buttermilk	250 mL
2 tbsp.	butter	30 mL
2-2½ cups	halved OR broken pecans	500-625 mL

In a large, heavy saucepan, combine the sugar and baking soda. Mix well. Add the buttermilk. Cook over high heat for 5 minutes or to 210°F (105°C) on a candy thermometer, being sure to stir frequently and to scrape bottom and sides of pan while stirring. Add butter and pecans. Continue to cook, stirring frequently and scraping bottom and sides of pan, until a little of the mixture forms a very soft ball in cold water, about 5 minutes or 230°F (115°C). Remove from heat. Beat with a spoon until thick and creamy. Immediately drop by tablespoons (15 mL) onto wax paper, aluminum foil or lightly greased cookie sheet.

Yield: 20 large or 30 small pralines.

Note: If candy becomes too stiff before dropping from spoon, add 1 tbsp. (15 mL) hot water and stir well.

Variation: Pour into a buttered 9 x 13" (23 x 33 cm) pan and slice when cool.

Combine a well-balanced diet with regular exercise.

Butter Tart Squares

This is a special family favorite. The squares are delicious, easy to make and freeze well if they last past mealtime! Super for entertaining.

Base

½ cup	butter OR margarine	125 mL
¼ cup	brown sugar	50 mL
1¼ cups	flour	300 mL

Filling

⅓ cup	butter	75 mL
2 tbsp.	buttermilk	30 mL
1 tsp.	vanilla	5 mL
1 cup	brown sugar (dark or light)	250 mL
1 tbsp.	flour	15 mL
1	egg, beaten	1
1 cup	raisins	250 mL

Prepare the base by creaming the butter and sugar together; then mix in the flour. Press the mixture into a 9 x 9" (23 x 23 cm) pan. Bake at 350°F (180°C) for 15 minutes. (For an extra-thick treat, use a smaller square pan.) Prepare the filling by mixing together the butter, buttermilk, vanilla, sugar and flour. Blend in the beaten egg. Add the raisins and mix thoroughly. Spread this mixture over the base. Bake at 275°F (140°C) for approximately 25 minutes. Do not overbake if you love juicy, runny squares as we do.

Yield: Approximately 36 squares.

Pumpkin Squares

Delightfully different! A great way to serve kids pumpkin and squash.

1½ cups	mashed, cooked pumpkin OR squash	375 mL
1½ cups	whole-wheat flour	375 mL
1 cup	firmly packed brown sugar	250 mL
1 tsp.	baking powder	5 mL
2 tsp.	cinnamon	10 mL
1 tsp.	ground ginger	5 mL
½ tsp.	nutmeg	2 mL
½ tsp.	baking soda	2 mL
¼ cup	buttermilk	50 mL
¼ cup	sunflower oil	50 mL
1 tsp.	vanilla	5 mL
2	eggs, well beaten	2
¼ cup	chopped nuts	50 mL

Combine all ingredients and beat with an electric mixer for 2-3 minutes at medium speed. Pour into a greased 9 x 13" (23 x 33 cm) pan, spread top as smoothly as you can and bake at 350°F (180°C) for about 30-40 minutes. Serve plain or ice with vanilla icing.

Yield: 24 squares.

Banana-Raspberry Trifle

	⅔ of a jelly roll OR ⅓ Yogurt Cake (see recipe, page 106) cut in 1" (2.5 cm) cubes	
6 oz.	sherry	175 mL
1 tbsp.	unflavored gelatin (1 pkg.)	15 mL
2 cups	raspberry juice (reserved juice plus extra for required amount) OR	500 mL
3 oz.	pkg. raspberry gelatin	85 g
14 oz.	can raspberries, drained (reserve juice)	398 mL
2	bananas, sliced	2
2½-3 cups	vanilla pudding OR custard OR 6 oz. (170 g) pkg. vanilla pudding	625-750 mL
1½ cups	sour cream OR yogurt	375 mL
2 cups	chilled whipping cream	500 mL
1-2 tbsp.	sugar	15-30 mL
1 tsp.	vanilla	5 mL
	maraschino cherries, nuts OR coconut for garnish	

Cover the bottom of a large glass bowl with jelly-roll or cake cubes. Pour the sherry over the cake. Prepare the unflavored gelatin per package directions using raspberry juice OR prepare the raspberry gelatin with 1 cup (250 mL) boiling water and 1 cup (250 mL) reserved raspberry juice. Pour over the cake. Leave to set. Add a layer of raspberries and a layer of banana slices. In a separate pan or bowl, prepare the pudding and then fold in the sour cream to make a smooth mixture. Pour over the fruit. Whip the cream; add sugar and vanilla. Spread the whipped cream completely over the top. Decorate with fruit, nuts and/or coconut. Refrigerate. Do not make sooner than 1 day before serving.

Serves: 16-20.

Caramel Rice Pudding with Raisins

A tangy, sweet pudding. Serve as is or with milk.

2 cups	cooked rice	500 mL
1 tsp.	vanilla	5 mL
1½ cups	buttermilk	375 mL
2	eggs, slightly beaten	2
½-1 cup	raisins	125-250 mL
⅔ cup	brown sugar	150 mL
½ tsp.	cinnamon OR to taste	2 mL
pinch	nutmeg	pinch

Combine all ingredients in a buttered casserole dish and stir. Bake at 350°F (180°C) for approximately 30-40 minutes. Stir and cool. Golden liquid will be absorbed by rice while cooling.

Serves: 4-6.

Skim milk and cultured buttermilk each contain 0.1% fat.

Buttermilk and skim milk contain approximately 90% water.

Yogurt-Baked Apples

A pleasantly different way to enjoy an old favorite.

4	apples, halved lengthwise and cored	4
1 tbsp.	lemon juice	15 mL
1 cup	yogurt	250 mL
¼ cup	brown sugar	50 mL
1 tsp.	flour (optional)	5 mL
1/8 tsp.	cinnamon	0.5 mL
pinch	nutmeg	pinch
	frozen blueberries	

Place the apples, skin side down, into a baking dish. Sprinkle with lemon juice. Mix the yogurt, brown sugar, flour, cinnamon and nutmeg. Pour over apples and top each apple half with 5 or 6 blueberries. Bake at 350°F (180°C) for approximately 20 minutes or until apple puffs slightly. Serve warm.

Serves: 8.

Wash all fruits and vegetables thoroughly before cooking or serving raw to remove any residue from pesticide sprays.

Fold sliced berries into plain or fruited yogurts.

Frozen Fruit Yogurt

This creamy light dessert is delicious made with sliced strawberries too.

5 oz.	cream cheese	140 g
½ cup	sifted icing sugar	125 mL
1 cup	yogurt	250 mL
⅓ cup	frozen apple juice concentrate (raspberry, lime, lemon, etc. will do also)	75 mL
½ cup	whipping cream	125 mL
1½-2 cups	mixed fruit salad OR 16 oz. (500 g) can fruit cocktail, drained	375-500 mL
¼ cup	shredded coconut	50 mL
¼ cup	toasted almonds	50 mL
	fresh fruit for garnish	

Beat cream cheese with sugar; add yogurt and juice concentrate. Whip cream and fold in. Stir in fruit. Spread in a 9 x 9" (23 x 23 cm) pan. Freeze until firm. Let stand for 10 minutes at room temperature before serving. Cut into serving pieces and sprinkle with coconut and almonds. Top with fresh fruit.

Yield: 9 — 3" (7 cm) squares.

Frosty Banana Yogurt

Tasty, nutritious and not too sweet.

2	frozen bananas, skins removed	2
1 cup	plain yogurt	250 mL
½ tsp.	vanilla (optional)	5 mL

Break bananas into pieces and place, along with the yogurt and vanilla, in a blender or food processor. Blend and enjoy as a shake or with a spoon. Try freezing and blending twice more for a frozen yogurt treat.

Serves: 1.

Variation: Replace bananas with 1 cup (250 mL) or more frozen raspberries, strawberries or blueberries.

See photograph on page 48A.

Buttermilk Ice Cream

An interesting, soft-textured ice cream.

4 cups	buttermilk	1 L
2 cups	whipping cream	500 mL
2 cups	sugar	500 mL
1 tbsp.	vanilla	15 mL

Mix all ingredients and pour into ice cream churn, process according to manufacturer's directions. Place in a storage container and then freeze. Serve as is or with fruit.

Yield: Approximately 8 cups (2 L).

Index

Index

*Note: References after each recipe title refer to the key ingredients, used in this recipe. (B) - buttermilk; (S) - sour cream and (Y) - yogurt.

Special Considerations

To help with planning and entertaining, we like to keep a record of any special likes, dislikes or allergies of friends and relatives.

Name	Special Considerations	Comments